UFOs & Mental Health

Book One:
A Briefing on the Phenomenon

All the best—
Bob Teets

UFOs & Mental Health

Book One:

A Briefing on the Phenomenon

by

Bob Teets

Headline Books, Inc..
P.O. Box 52
Terra Alta, WV 26764
E-mail: TerraAlta@AOL.com

ISBN 0929915216

P r i n t e d   I n   C a n a d a

Acknowledgments

This book would not have been possible without the love, support and the sometimes heroic efforts of my wife, Cathy Teets. Thanks, too, to our friends and families around the many campfires we've shared during the summer of 1997—your very presence and love, the warmth of your friendship, the exquisite sounds of our children at play, all affirms life as it is meant to be. Kudos and acknowledgment, too, to W. H. Bowart, Dick Farley and David Ritchey, a threesome who came through on a tight deadline without complaint, and to Donna Higbee for her invaluable contribution.

Dedication

To teachers everywhere from an inquisitive student. And to Diana, Deborah, David, Doctor Bill, Farley, Bowart, Mahlon (wherever you are), and most especially my Dad—the explorers. And to Richard and Ashley—the future.

Table of Contents

UFOs and Mental Health
Book One:
A Briefing on the Phenomenon

Introduction

This isn't an end-all book about UFOs and mental health, it's a beginning, a primer so to speak that I hope will spark interest in this subject from within the mental health community. I hope this approach will provide a viable framework on which to begin building a database and providing a forum for honest, open, democratic discussion of a most unusual and apparently burgeoning phenomenon. In that regard, it's a work in progress, and once healers* review this book, I trust they will begin to think of their own practices and experiences in hopes of eventually building a corpus of information helpful to all others positively involved in the profession. Thus, I envision more books in the future, as we begin to accumulate more and more therapeutic data and finely tuned approaches to helping clients unravel their problems.

This isn't to suggest that there haven't been excellent books and much work already or about to be published in this area. We must, therefore, fully and gratefully acknowledge the contributions of colleagues who've been on the front lines, as they have helped to lift the veil for a peek into this enigmatic phenomenon. You will find their work in the bibliography. Except for Leo Sprinkle's. Particular and sincere acknowledgment of this pioneer counseling psychologist's efforts must be noted here. Dr. Leo Sprinkle, now Professor Emeritus, Counseling Services at the University of Wyoming, has gone where no therapist has gone before. His efforts to scientifically investigate the phenomenon from the viewpoint of a mental health professional began in the early 1960s, and in my opinion he is still the best investigator we have in the mental health field. In addition to his keen insight and significant contributions via research, Leo has for years managed a brain child of his called the Rocky Mountain UFO Conference at the University of Wyoming, and has thus provided a safe forum for percipients of the phenomenon to share their feelings and to heal together. The conference continues with Leo now serving in the capacity of what should be labeled "Pioneer Emeritus." The conference was a labor of love. But then, Dr. Sprinkle seems to have no limits in that regard. And no limit to his infectious mirth either. Simply put, if this field is to move forward in any positive way, it will not be able to do so without full acknowledgment of Leo's incredible contributions. Luckily for us all, he has written a book that is due out in the

Spring of 1998—*Soul Samples: Personal Explorations of Reincarnation and UFO Experiences (*which will be available from Wildflower Press, P. O. Box 190, Mill Spring, NC 28756). I can think of no book I'd rather read. Writing it must been have like trying to write the UFO equivalent of *War and Peace,* a massive undertaking. Leo deserves an entire library section all to himself. To this day, Dr. Sprinkle demonstrates the only effective way of helping percipients to explore their experiences, by offering them "unqualified positive acceptance" as a first course. He continues to work with percipients in his small Laramie, Wyoming office. To borrow a thought from an Irish minister I once heard: If there is a heaven, and if in the far twilight of a far distant future Leo Sprinkle is denied access to it, I don't even want to aspire to it.

With all deference to these pioneers, especially to Dr. Sprinkle, I believe some areas of the UFO phenomenon have been unintentionally downplayed when they write about it, namely because these folks are healers and not day-to-day journalists. They are, however, fully aware of the broad range of possibilities needed for a thorough examination of the UFO phenomenon—a fact which contributes mightily to their effectiveness as therapists.

And that's where I see this book coming in, as a briefing to help expand your own understanding of the phenomenon, just in case you haven't been studying it sincerely for over 30 years, like Leo Sprinkle.

Even though I'm no longer a member of the working press and am now a book publisher, I remain a journalist at heart, namely because I have more questions than answers about the subject of UFOs, questions which I regard with as much delight and self-satisfaction as you perhaps regard the degree initials appearing behind your name on the office door or on your stationery or business card. With the subject of UFOs, science journalism becomes "interstitial journalism," a specialty one does not necessarily seek but which, like the phenomenon itself, sometimes bestows itself on a person without invitation or preparation. And the longer one toils in this sort of journalism the finer the questions become, as if they are being smelted and purified by the fiery white-hot tail of an elusive curiosity on the periphery of consciousness. And since there are few, if any, degrees granted in UFOs—not that anyone would seek such a thing—there are at least serious and important considerations associated with the phenomenon that directly impact mental health. Thus comes a perceived need for a bridge of information between the phenomenon and the mental health professionals charged with helping some percipients to cope.

There is a personal component to all of this, too, in that I once spotted a UFO during a brief and intense experience in my childhood. I often reflect back to that dreamy summer morning of nearly 40 years ago on our remote West Virginia farm and wonder, as is common of most UFO "experiencers," if what I saw was "real." The journalist in me allows for several explanations of that long-ago event, and I am comfortable with keeping the memory and potential implications of it in a perpetual stasis while embracing the ambiguity of an enormously confusing and ofttimes anxiety ridden phenomenon. Receiving certification as a hypnotherapist and becoming more familiar with altered states of consciousness have certainly offered meaningful help to me in this regard. But it's also complicated an already complicated story, as you will see.

Being somewhat of a late bloomer and having a first child at the age of 40 has perhaps been the most help of all, since in the eyes of our now 7-year-old daughter is an infectious, wide-eyed, unquestioning, unqualified sense of joy—obtained simply by being! Perhaps this is the essence of the human survival instinct, and the place where surely everyone, including ourselves and our clients alike, would love to function day to day.

I have included in this primer some excerpts of personal essays, highlights of some presentations I've given over time, and some opinion and analysis. However, this is not to suggest that I offer definitive answers. It is a briefing of available research gleaned from top researchers in the world, one of whom has contributed heavily to this book. Dick Farley would not care for me to go on at length about him, would indeed probably rebel at any mention of him at all other than perhaps as a journalist and policy analyst, so I will restrain myself to a simple declarative sentence: When it comes to a breadth and depth of knowledge about this phenomenon and its implications, there is none better. I also borrow some understanding of the mental health aspects of the phenomenon from W. H. Bowart, a first rate journalist, successful author and mental health activist.

All this in an attempt to give you a briefing, just as I would if I were attempting to fulfill an assignment from an inquisitive news editor. Since I have employed hypnosis with only a small number of clients regarding their perceived difficulties with UFOs, while at the same time having interviewed hundreds of UFO eyewitnesses, I continue to view the phenomenon more as a journalist than as a healer. I'm counting on you to help me fill in the therapeutic side over time in future volumes.

The UFO phenomenon, as you will see, probably has very little to do with aliens and exotic space ships visiting earth and interacting with humans, though one is always hesitant to discount the possibility that such events have happened or are occurring now. Based on interviews I've conducted with approximately 2,500 eyewitnesses who've reported UFO experiences to me, there is certainly no way I will sweep my hand over them and declare them all to be suffering some psychological malady or a briefly popular psychosis and let it go at that. No way.

Instead, what I will commit to is a notion of a quantum reality that far surpasses the strangest offerings of science fiction and of science "fact." In truth, the UFO phenomenon may not be so much about what's *out there,* as it is about human consciousness and all of its associated mysteries and foibles. But the *out there* is an influencing factor as much as any other. Such a broad outlook may well include the possibility of "nonhuman" intelligence interfacing with us, the intelligence clearly capable of manifesting in varying ways, sometimes in exotic flying machines, sometimes in a non-linear-non-local mode, sometimes in spiritual ways, and sometimes in more archetypal ways, including even in the guise of familiar angels, demons and other critters. There is also, literature suggests, an identifiable "dark side" to the UFO phenomenon which appears for everything to be a combination of human and "other," a relationship perhaps sparked in the interstitial spaces of our existence and dated as early as the beginning of our species. And there is an equal if not immensely superior "good" side to the phenomenon, as well.

But the phenomenon also has to do with the possibility of quite human-driven experiences and, often, of manipulation of other humans' perceptions. In our 3-D reality, the human element as sometimes both perpetrator and experiencer is the most important component of the phenomenon.

And there are also other components of physiological, spiritual, philosophical, mythological, sociological and even of *political* flavorings to add to the mix.

Interestingly, and according to at least one survey conducted by Brad Steiger and Sherry Hansen Steiger,[1] the typical "experiencer's" profile may closely match your own! The Steiger's say those most prone to filling out their "Star People Questionnaire" (relating to perceived paranormal experiences) are people who consider themselves "helpers" in our society, such as "schoolteachers, nurses, social workers, psychic counselors, psychologists, college professors, college students, high school students, law enforcement officers and members of the clergy," to name a few.

Without a doubt, people often do perceive within their consciousness something extraordinary. And if they walk in through the door of your office and indicate to you an association of their personal problems with their extraordinary "experiences," then you may well need extraordinary ways of helping them.

I hope this book is a start in that regard.

Bob Teets
September, 1997

(*Please note, I make no distinction between "mainstream" or "alternative" mental health practitioners, clinicians, counselors, clergy, hypnotherapists and others, and thus prefer the generically respectful term "healers" or, when necessary, the more generalized term "therapists.")

(1. *Star Born,* Brad Steiger and Sherry Hansen Steiger, 1992, Berkley Books, New York)

Chapter One

UFO Reality? There Isn't One!

Right here, right now in our 3-D existence on earth, all we collectively know about UFOs is that they are about various, sometimes competing, human beliefs.

If you are a healer, you may occasionally find a client who wishes to explore what s/he perceives as past UFO experiences. And if you are a UFO "experiencer" in search of answers to or relief from perceived problems associated with UFOs, you will often discover that the answers you find and/or the degree of relief you experience may well depend on which healer you choose. It can all be quite confusing for both the healer and the experiencer because each of you may find yourself mired in a sticky array of belief systems...including your own! It's little wonder, because when you compile a broad listing, you will find belief systems ranging from known government and military complicity to new science and exotic technology, from philosophy to archangelic realms, and from interstitial spaces to planetary consciousness.

It's a bewildering mix. And there are many, many believers advocating for each system.

Here's an example:

A Brief Example:

Say a client reports to you disturbing experiences involving abduction by UFO occupants/aliens. Based upon available research, here is a sample list of potential causes of the client's experience (please note—these are not ranked according to importance, nor is this a comprehensive listing):

A. S/he was abducted by aliens.

B. S/he was the subject of human or "other," or a combination of human and other-sponsored mind control experiment(s) or programs and/or related ritual-oriented and/or related accelerated learning scenarios—and was, via intense trauma-based programming and/or induced amnesia (possibly including a combination of intense hypnosis and/or psychoactive drug and/or electroshock and/or internal/external electromagnetic and/or other "non-lethal" means) or by other means "implanted" with "cover memories" to convince him/her of an alien abduction scenario.

C. S/he was convinced of an abduction experience by another therapist or third party (regardless of motivation), or perhaps by exposure to wide media coverage of "UFOs" or entertainment vehicles (books, movies, etc.).

D. S/he experienced, whether intentionally or not, an intense psycho-spiritual episode which could have been self-induced or triggered by human, supra-human, or non-human intelligence which s/he interpreted as—or was convinced or coerced into believing was—connected to "UFO aliens."

E. S/he experienced another kind of paranormal event (voluntary/involuntary accessing of the "collective unconscious," spontaneous out-of-body scenario, a "channeling" event, spirit possession, etc.) which s/he interpreted as alien abduction.

F. S/he is experiencing one or more psychological disorders.

G. S/he is otherwise culturally predisposed to interpreting some potentially troubling or traumatic events as being connected to alien abduction. (There is little literature to directly affirm this possibility, though one can draw at least an oblique connection from a mention in the DSM of cultural predisposition to certain psycho-spiritual conditions, such as spirit possession.)

There are other possibilities you can probably enumerate, of course (and certainly the potential exists to combine any or all of the above), but this list suffices to illustrate my points:

1. that throughout history and throughout our society, there is evidence to support each of the above categories;

2. and that, given equal weight to each separate possibility, there is at best a one in seven chance of any particular category adequately portraying your client's condition.

Kind of puts a whole new spin on the importance of proper diagnosis, doesn't it?

The Matrix

A few years ago I worked as a consulting editor/researcher for the non-profit Human Potential Foundation, Inc. (HPF) in Falls

Church, Virginia. HPF's mission was to study ways of bridging so-called "New Science" with more traditional scientific modalities. Exciting research was occurring in areas of inter-species communication, consciousness, life-after-death, non-human intelligence and alternative energy sources, all of which the Foundation wanted to examine and to then aid via scientific research in whatever ways seemed possible. When I first joined HPF, I was surprised to learn that all of these areas under investigation were connected in some ways with another subject the Foundation was studying—UFOs! The primary funding source for the HPF, Laurance Rockefeller of New York, recognized these connections and was attempting to encourage governmental openness regarding the UFO phenomenon as part of an overall plan to examine these areas, he said. This gave rise to a presidential briefing paper (see below) that can now help you to identify belief systems and to then use that knowledge in ways to possibly benefit your clients.

The following "Matrix" document, then, is the essence of a briefing paper prepared for President Clinton and presented in 1993 to his science advisor, Dr. John Gibbons. It was written by my former HPF colleague and journalist friend C. Richard Farley, Jr., and remains to this day the best and most comprehensive thumbnail overview of the UFO phenomenon I've seen.

Note that when considering the following you should first take into account your client's belief, then compare and contrast it with the following:

Human Potential Foundation
UFO Matrix of "Belief"

The following is a matrix of the spectrum of scenarios found in current literature which are used to try to explain so-called UFO or ETI activity, or the lack thereof. Each matrix entry has a supporting constituency. Some of these constituencies are quite vocal, but no less confident that their current belief structures are the most reasonable, given the data which are generally accepted. There most certainly is a large minority which is not willing to commit to one matrix entry over another, or in combination, until additional data are available. For years, opinion polls have consistently measured that a comfortable majority of the American public believes in the reality of UFOs and Extraterrestrial Intelligence.

0. All sightings except for a small minority which lack detail can be explained in terms of naturally occurring phenomena.

1. Craft from "off planet," but from the visible universe.

2. Interdimensional penetrations by other intelligences or life-forms, based in or operating from another (parallel) overlapping dimension than our own "time-space."

3. Earth-based "others," referenced throughout history, who may be other life-forms, or predominately resident in realms or dimensions we term "spiritual."

4. Hoaxes or "dramatic" scenarios perpetrated by various intelligence organizations as part of broader security or disinformation campaigns.

5. Broader "social engineering," or population mind-influencing programs, designed to promote a more "universal" planetary consciousness and to reduce the influence of nationalistic or religious traditions.

6. Any combination of the above, including "all of the above." Intent: unknown.

Possible U.S. Government levels of awareness, involvement and/or "control" of the phenomena termed "UFO."

0. No activity, inasmuch as the phenomena are explained by naturally occurring events.

1. Aware, but not directly involved or in contact with the perpetrating forces.

2. In contact to some degree, and "co-operating" with at least some of the source-phenomena or intelligences, either for technology trading or because government believes it has no choice.

3. Government is the perpetrator of at least some of the phenomenology, perhaps drawing on the source experience for ideas and methods, but employing the events for other purposes, such as intelligence, disinformation or to alarm other nations.

4. At least some UFO phenomena are results of government or other agency sponsored experiments in "mind-

control," or "social control" experiments or initiatives.

PLEASE NOTE: The Human Potential Foundation, Inc. does not endorse any of the entries of the preceding Matrix of Belief. The Matrix has been prepared to stimulate discussion and research into the broad spectrum of ideas that are represented in current literature addressing what are popularly known as UFO phenomena.

DISCUSSION

Matrix of UFO Beliefs was designed to be a multifaceted investigative tool

by Dick Farley
<cloudrider@aol.com>

WASHINGTON, DC - In October, 1992, philanthropist Laurance S. Rockefeller asked the Human Potential Foundation, Inc., (HPF) to staff his UFO declassification initiative to the White House.

I had been hired as the director of project development for the HPF, chaired by Rhode Island's U. S. Senator Claiborne Pell, a close friend of Mr. Rockefeller's who also was serving at that time as Chairman of the Senate Foreign Relations Committee.

In turn, Laurance Rockefeller was at that juncture essentially our "sole source" benefactor, helping Senator Pell and HPF's president, Dr. C. B. "Scott" Jones, Jr., get the foundation up and active. We were developing a spectrum of program initiatives designed to bring exotic or emergent new scientific paradigms into closer and more objective evaluations by "establishment" disciplines than "new science" had usually received in the past.

My task in support of our White House UFO disclosure effort was to recommend and produce background materials for Mr. Rockefeller to leave behind after his meeting to make his case. One of these documents HPF later sent to White House Science Advisor, Dr. John Gibbons, was the *Matrix of UFO Beliefs*, on which I had been working long before signing on with the HPF.

The *Matrix of UFO Beliefs* is an investigative and analytical tool that had its genesis during my 20 years of active inquiry into "UFO" phenomena. It reflects primary categories into which beliefs about UFOs seem to fall, when allowing for the broadest range of reported phenomena and perceptions.

Contributors to my thinking included Dr. J. Allen Hynek, in a series of conversations we had (1981 to 1984), as well as Dr. Jacques Vallee, who played an early consultative role in what HPF did to support Mr. Rockefeller's interest in UFO disclosure.

Diversity and apparent divergence of various UFO-related experiences are relatively well-represented in the *Matrix of UFO Beliefs*, because it does not require immediate exclusions and preconditions before a belief or "causality" is considered.

The *Matrix of UFO Beliefs* was not designed to suggest to the President or his advisors what "all the UFOs might be." And the paper reflects my assumption that, for at least some publicly perceived "UFOs," various of our government's branches would be expected to know very well what may have been witnessed.

Primarily, the *Matrix of UFO Beliefs* was to serve us as our outline for a briefing of the President and his senior advisors on the range of public opinions and beliefs about UFOs as had been determined from: the popular literature; activity at UFO conferences; and throughout respective UFO venues into which beliefs evolved or had been seeded, manipulated or reinforced.

The second part of the *Matrix of UFO Beliefs* is reflective of our assessment (5/14/93) of the range of citizen beliefs about what our government might know, and what roles its agencies may have been or be playing. These analyses I also arrived at by sifting through most of the organizational venues of "UFOlogy."

Mr. Rockefeller's first meeting on this matter was with White House Science Advisor, Dr. John Gibbons, in mid-April, 1993. It had been preceded by an exchange of preparatory letters among Mr. Rockefeller; then-Defense Secretary-designate Les Aspin; Rockefeller friend and former (Nixon era) Secretary of Defense Melvin Laird; the Rev. Dr. Billy Graham, and important others.

Mr. Rockefeller had invited some of these men to "sign on" to his proposed UFO disclosure letter to President Bill Clinton. HPF's staffers and consultants joined with Mr. Rockefeller's advisors in drafting and revising this letter, both before Laurance's meeting with Dr. Gibbons and during HPF's subsequent support.

The *Matrix of UFO Beliefs* was delivered to Dr. Gibbons at

the White House in mid-May, 1993, along with a dozen selected popular books about the UFO phenomena that had been chosen (by me) to be representative of the various UFO beliefs as my document reflected, as outlined in its annotated bibliography.

Mr. Rockefeller's second meeting on this matter, along with Dr. Jones and Washington attorney Henry L. Diamond, was with Dr. Gibbons and several White House staff members, Feb. 4, 1994.

If you use your own knowledge of human psychology/altered states of consciousness and then open your current belief system to incorporate and to overlay this *Matrix*, you may well discover a dynamic new structure capable of helping you to help your clients in more meaningful ways.

Chapter Two

Possibilities

Bringing the Matrix to Life

Sometimes the hardest part about considering this phenomenon is keeping an open mind while exploring its depths. It's so full of variables, and it is quite accommodating of those willing to believe in limited facets of it. In that regard, it may be a good idea to follow the advice of another true explorer like yourself, oceanographer Jacques-Yves Cousteau*:

"Don't be a slave to your own beliefs."

That's the real beauty of the *Matrix* (see Chapter 1). While it may be a pretty radical document, given that it went into the White House through the front door while purporting the possibility of alien life forms along with some prosaic and some troubling alternatives, it certainly allows us to examine the BROADEST outlines of the phenomenon without needing to settle on any particular belief.

Why is that important?

First of all, and as we most recently witnessed in March, 1997, UFO related belief systems—even ones that look at first like they're somewhat bizarre but harmless— can kill.

The web page logo of the Heaven's Gate group, formerly known as Total Overcomers Anonymous (TOA), and prior to that as Human Individual Metamorphosis (HIM)

Heaven's Gate: Opinion and Analysis of a UFO-related Suicide

There could not be a more stark and somber reminder of the sometimes toxic nature of UFO-related belief systems than the mass suicide of the Heaven's Gate group in California on March 26, 1997.

Amid the sensational racket and roar of media coverage of the event, one voice did sound through to touch on the truth of the matter. Reflecting on the group's apparent shared belief in the appearance of Comet Hale-Bopp as heralding a time for group members to shed their "earthly containers" in order to join a UFO accompanying the comet— astronomer David Levy said in an Associated Press (AP) interview, "The comet doesn't do the killing. It's the beliefs that do."

The April 14, 1997 edition of People Weekly *concentrated on the backgrounds of "39 ordinary people" who committed mass suicide March 26. "Though some of those who joined Heaven's Gate had obvious emotional problems," the lead article stated, "most seemed disarmingly ordinary—businessmen, mothers, students—all consumed by nothing more exotic than a desire for spiritual enlightenment."*

People Weekly hit on part of an explanation, I think, when its lead article included this observation: "Though some of those who joined Heaven's Gate had obvious emotional problems, most seemed disarmingly ordinary—businessmen, mothers, students—all consumed by nothing more exotic than a desire for spiritual enlightenment."[1]

That was a powerful statement in *People Weekly*, especially when you consider the innocence with which most of us at sometime in our lives feel compelled to step onto a path of discovery for ourselves, a path which will lead in part and inevitably toward things spiritual. More and more, it seems, people are seeking spiritual knowledge.

So, how was it that 39 people, many if not most of them average or above average in intelligence or creativity, narrowed their options over time to the point where a belief in suicide appeared to be the best choice available to them?

For sure, one method by which a choice can be made like the Heaven's Gate clan is to engage in a society where life is increasingly viewed as a commodity with little value, meaning or relevance.

As an example, you have the option of joining the opinion of a few rich, elite "personalities" on the American scene who commented on the Heaven's Gate suicides. Billionaire Ted Turner, the founder of Turner Broadcasting (CNN, etc.) and owner of the Atlanta Braves baseball team said a few days after the suicide that the event was "a good way to get rid of a few nuts," as reported by AP and *The New York Post*. A bit later, he added, "There's too many people anyway." Millionaire Jay Leno, a corporate comedian, managed to milk humor from the incident on his April 2 "Tonight Show." Others have since followed suit.

There is no doubt that Turner and Leno are in the positions they hold in order to help anesthetize the public, to aid us in considering the suicidal deaths of 39 people as a positive way of reducing the population or as funny.

Another way of considering the 39 deaths, though, is to think of Heaven's Gate followers as being far more human than either the media tycoon or the corporate funny man who make their riches precisely because of their inhumanity.

Examine the culture at large and you begin to see disturbing trends everywhere which key in on what Pope John Paul II has termed "the culture of death." New ways of killing and of inciting contempt for life are seeping into the popular consciousness through what one may infer from the Pope's 1995 encyclical letter entitled *The Gospel of Life* (*see bibliography for this and other books that are not excerpted or footnoted) as a long term and intentional manipulation of belief systems. In most cases, the subtlety and seduction of these beliefs are apparent only by careful examination.

For sure, events like this will make—or should make—people think twice about any "revealed truths" perpetrated by supposed UFO experts, believers or prophets. From now on, and in order to lead people in any march toward "UFO truth," these UFO myth perpetrators and prophets will surely have to convince their followers to keep their "eyes on the skies" while ignoring beneath them the dead bodies of 39 more followers over whom they must tread.

But it has happened before.

Since 1994, a total of 74 people connected with the Solar Temple cult in Switzerland and Canada have committed murder and suicide in the name of UFOs—five of them just days prior to the Heaven's Gate deaths, according to *USA Today*.[2]

Not too many years ago, in 1978, a popular and charismatic New Age apostle and UFO proponent named Ira Einhorn, known to insiders as "The Unicorn," was convicted of murder *in abstentia* for chopping up his girlfriend, Holly Maddux, in his suburban

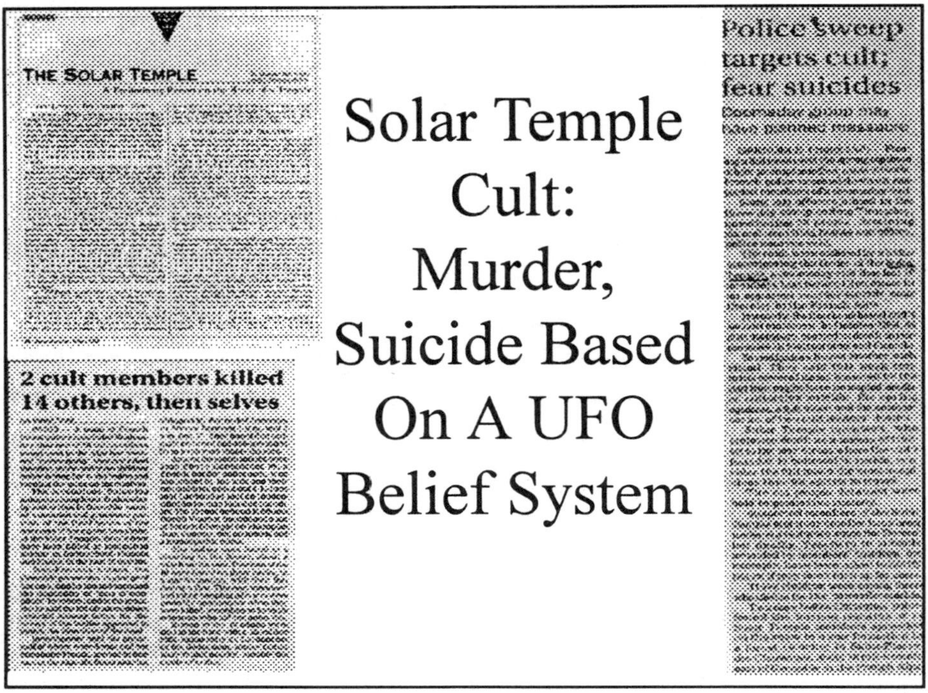

Philadelphia apartment. Einhorn insisted he had been framed by intelligence agencies who feared he knew too much about technology, some of which apparently formed the basis of mind control weapons. The Unicorn is now believed to be in custody in France and awaiting extradition after skipping bail and hiding out in Europe for nearly two decades. The question now is—since Einhorn's phalanx of followers and associates once included some of the most elite names in the U.S. and Canada—will he be allowed to live long enough to be returned to this country? It would seem, if Einhorn's aliens of which he spoke so eloquently in the 1970s and 1980s are real, that now would be the time for them to race in and rescue Ira before somebody powers up the electric chair (or the mind control assassin team), else the shock of his revelations could send a jolt to the highest echelons of American, Canadian and even of European elite society.

In another case, this one from only a few years ago, Robert Joe Moody was convicted of murdering two women. Throughout his trial, according to early coverage of the event by W. H. Bowart (for more on this journalist, see Chapter 6), Moody insisted he had been told to kill the women by space aliens. In exchange for following the aliens' orders and being put to death because of his crime, Moody said, the aliens promised to resurrect him after his execution.

There are many—*many*—more instances of murders and suicides perpetrated in the name of or connected with UFOs, though these should suffice to illustrate the point. These cases push us close to the heart of the UFO phenomenon, in that they cross many of the same psychological bounds with which a therapist must deal on a daily basis. And they demonstrate the need for an open mind because the possible influences on these human perpetrators and suicide victims could range across the entire *Matrix of UFO Beliefs*, from the metaphysical to the mind controlled.

So, whether singly or in multitudes, the corpses pile up. In fact, and while noting his own personal shock of such events, retired Air Force Major and UFO author *(Unmasking the Enemy,)* Nelson Pacheco, sharing in the Pope's cultural perspective, once commented (and I'm paraphrasing here), "If you want to do UFO research, one clear way is to follow the trail of bodies." His meaning presumably included both those who commit suicide or are killed as a result of their association with UFO and related phenomena, **as well as those who are mentally destabilized as a result of that association**. (This is not to exclude those whose mental problems preceded their entry into the UFO field!) Conservative

Christian author Dave Hunt makes a similar point in his now classic bestselling novel, *The Archon Conspiracy*.

Many secular opinions agree on several aspects of the point, as well. A former CIA official who reportedly is quite interested in studying such belief systems has noted that at least some of these types of toxic beliefs are quite possibly of a variety that we could conceive of as an information virus that acts similar to a biological virus by infecting its host on levels sometimes unnoticed for years or decades, but which definitely alters the host's

behavior and attitude from the time it first enters the host's body (brain). Author Richard Brodie examines the so-called new science of "memetics" in his book, *Virus of the Mind*. Defense industry consultants, "non-lethal weapons" experts and science fiction authors Chris and Janet Morris echo the idea of infection of humans by a biological / information virus in their book, *The Stalk*. (Janet Morris, it must noted, is also credited as a co-author of *Window of Opportunity: A Blueprint For The Future*, a 1984 book by The Hon. Newt Gingrich.)

Newsweek columnist Geoffrey Cowley, writing about the new science of memetics, was right on the mark when he wrote:

> "...a virus that kills its host doesn't always kill itself. ... if even a small minority of the TV viewers now following the Heaven's Gate story responded to the cult's message, the message might survive."[3]

And so may its affects.

Other Possibilities

H.I.S.S.

An interesting idea is beginning to emerge based on continuing work performed by one researcher with whom I've conversed: People who are unusually prone to having alien abduction experiences "and other transpersonal experiences" can be thought of as being *sensitive* to "alternate realities."

David Ritchey, Ph.D., working with a paper and pencil test instrument entitled the "Holistic Inventory of Stimulus Sensitivities" sees preliminary indications (the full results of the test won't be known for some time) that these individuals may have a variety of unusual sensitivities in the physiological, immunological, neurological and psychological realms.

Dr. Ritchie speaks of these people as "anomalously sensitive persons" and points out that a sensitivity to "or proneness to entering" alternate states of consciousness seems to be the common thread which connects all of the different manifestations of anomalous sensitivity. "Indications are," he states, "that presenting symptoms (in the clinical context) which suggest such things as alien abduction experiences, stress related illnesses, developmental learning disorders, and post traumatic stress disorder are not as different as they might at first appear to be." At its root, he suggests, each issue appears to have its genesis in an alternate state of consciousness that is working to the detriment of rather than to the benefit of the client.

"If the 'illing' originates in an alternate state of consciousness," he suggests, "then that's where the 'healing' is going to occur." This is "state dependent learning" in reverse, he says. If a dysfunctional learning occurred in a specific state of consciousness, then that state of consciousness has to be recreated for an "unlearning" to occur.

Moreover, whether or not a particular problem or issue seems to be "really real" (i.e., a part of consensual reality) should be of no particular import to the psychotherapist, he seems to assert. "What is important in this work is the subjective reality of the client, and the therapist needs to join the client in that reality 'as if' it were 'really real' in order for the psychotherapy to be effective."

SRT

In the realm of possibilities, too, are the "dark others" that are said to inculcate themselves into human consciousness. These are variously referred to as "demons" in the classic Judeo-Christian literature, as "jinn" by Muslim writers, or as the negative aspect of "trickster" by Native American Indian storytellers. These energies, whatever they are, are known by other names in different cultures and across all human time, as well.

In his book, *Spirit Releasement Therapy: A Technique Manual,* ** William J. Baldwin, D.D.S., Ph.D., lays out an approach to dealing with these energies using a unique modality he developed over years of practice with clients in his counseling practice. One of the traits Baldwin sees in many of his clients, and which he writes about in his book, is a sort of possession of a human being by an interstitial extraterrestrial-type entity. Where it gets interesting is at the point where this extraterrestrial is found to itself be possessed by a classic demon, or jinn.

Let's take a minute and review a little more in-depth the "demon factor" of the UFO phenomenon.

(*as quoted to me by Cousteau's one-time policy analyst, Dick Farley, yes, the same guy who wrote the *Matrix of UFO Beliefs* featured in Chapter 1)

(1. *People Weekly,* Vol. 47, No. 14, April 14, 1997)

(2. *USA Today*, March 28, 1997, Page 12A)

(3. *Newsweek,* 4/14/97 The Millennium/Departments/Viruses of the Mind: How Odd Ideas Survive)

(**I'm familiar with Dr. Baldwin's material because I've trained in his methods and my company publishes his book. Coming soon will *CE VI: Close Encounters of the Clinical Kind,* in which Dr. Baldwin further examines the relationship between SRT and ETs.)

Chapter Three

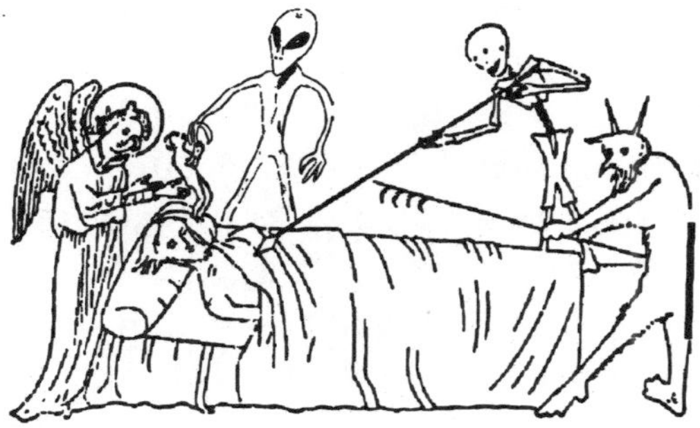

Spirit Possession and Alien Abduction: Similarities of an Enigma

Just for the record, you won't find much mention of spirit possession in the *DSM*, other than, perhaps, as a factor related to a dissociative, fantasy-prone personality or disorder, or as a predisposition to the beliefs of a limited number of indigenous peoples. And so far, I'm not familiar with any insurance companies which cover against spirit possession or which reimburse expenses for exorcism. It's a shame, really, since in this realm of UFOs, spirit possession seems as much a possibility in at least some cases as does any other indicator. As we just saw suggested in the previous chapter, perhaps one way of addressing this is for the therapist to suspend personal belief systems and to work within the client's "reality."

I cannot unequivocally state that so-called demons or extraterrestrials are, in fact, objectively real. But as I continue to research subjects seemingly connected with the UFO phenomenon, it is apparent from a great number of percipients I've interviewed (and collateral research, as well) that the net effects of many, but certainly not all, of these interactions—be they with non-human intelligences or with other states of mind (i.e. consciousness and all of its variations and aberrations)— appear to demonstrate many similarities between the UFO abduction experience and demonic/spirit possession.

This is not to eliminate other possibilities (as we recall the "Matrix of UFO Beliefs" in Chapter 1), but for the purposes of this chapter, I will concentrate on this single aspect of the phenomenon.

While also not attempting to present a conclusive epistemological examination (and clearly I am not suggesting this to be anything but perhaps a glimpse of part of an interesting phenomenon that contains many more elements than those addressed here), I can identify the following similarities between alien abduction and spirit possession.

"The Fallen Lucifer" (After Dore)— from *The History of the Devil*

How They Operate

I. Examine the fear factor: most people would find it equally abhorrent to either be abducted from their bedrooms by aliens and to have various traumatizing experiments/molestations perpetrated against them, or to be possessed by a demon or discarnate, in either case to be powerless to stop the intrusive activities. However, it is observable, at least from having interviewed many percipients, and having read the UFO literature, that <u>many percipients would rather admit to or at least consider alien interference in their lives than to consider demon possession</u>, the former offering some modicum of contact, perhaps with higher intelligence (in the extreme, perhaps, as Harvard psychiatrist John Mack, M.D. and a long list of others opine, contact with messengers of God), while the latter denotes "unclean," morally corrupting contact (and perhaps even cooperation) with the ultimate evil force in the universe.

II. We can at least partially judge these entities by their affects on people.

III. Those who are abducted report never being the same again, as if their alien abductors were always nearby or, in some cases, within them (much like an infection or a possession state). Dr. William J. Baldwin, author of *Spirit Releasement Therapy: A Technique Manual*, assisted by his wife, Rev. Judith Baldwin, often refer to dark entities like this:

"They are simply bacteria, no more, no less. They are another life form with a different purpose. What right do bacteria have to join our bodies?"

The Baldwins' statement infers consciousness as inherent with these entities.

IV. Many modern researchers are now saying that abductees are finding their experiences more and more acceptable, even

A stylized drawing of Satan. Note the similarities of the various disc shapes on the amulet with those of UFO-type vehicles. —from *The History of the Devil.*

spiritually uplifting and transformational. Social worker John Carpenter, director of abduction research for the Mutual UFO Network (MUFON), has noted a more accepting attitude in contactees/abductees. Dr. John Mack says many abductees come to love their alien captors. Author Whitley Strieber admits to his love and longing for the creatures (which had previously subjected him, without anesthetic, to medical-like experiments, including nasal and anal probes). In the case of spirit/demon possession, a large measure of the entities' success in the host depends on the host's cooperation. If the host finds power, profit or even love as a result of the visitors within (once they are recognized), then the host will naturally find the visitors' presence more and more acceptable, often even transformational in the broadest sense, to the point of developing a love for and/or a dependency on them. (The Stockholm Syndrome, recognized in victims of terrorist-like captivity, is seemingly overlooked by these researchers.)

V. Often, the ETs and spirit entities present themselves to percipients in identical ways.

VI. There are many cases where percipients are unable to separate the identities of these entities as being one or the other, ET or demon, which suggests that the entities, at least some of them, may be one and the same. (Conversely, many percipients confuse entities' identities with ETs and angels, as well.)

VII. In addition, both sets of entities are or seem capable of—

1. —telepathic communication

2. —hypnotic / altered state induction, regression, suggestion

3. —"hiding," both in the sense of successfully convincing the host /percipient to deny their existence AND at convincing a huge portion of the public that they don't exist. Also, both are capable of hiding in the physical sense, as well, within the layered psyche and often within the "physical"—or quantum or interstitial— body of the host.

4. —reprisal when discovered, often in equal measure to the level of emotional distress caused by the discovery

5. —time travel

6. —obtaining some measure of physical and mental control over their subjects for extended periods

7. —cajoling, manipulating, or in some way forcing their subjects to perform acts against the subjects' wills, including forced sexual intercourse (rape), violent crime, and suicide. The Solar Temple cult could be an extreme example of this concept: Leader Luc Jouret claimed contact with ETs, and said the only way to go to their planet was through the "Glory of Fire," which resulted in the fiery deaths and in some cases murder of known cult members in 1994 and more recently.

8. —physically moving their subjects from one location to another through various means, including a compromise of the percipient's free will through mind control / manipulation

9. —interacting with percipients/hosts at the "soul level"

10. —establishing highly organized, hierarchic networks capable of interacting with and controlling to some degree vast numbers of minions and human beings simultaneously

11. —according to Dr. Gregory Little, a psychologist and UFO researcher/author, these entities, at least the ones who do harm to human percipients, enter or manifest into the human perceptual levels from the lower frequencies of the electromagnetic spectrum (per his book, *Grand Illusions*)

12. —interrupting the transitory journey of the soul after death. Examples can be found in the Bible, in the book *Matrix II* (per the Nexus Group), various works by Maurice Rawlings (*To Hell and Back*), et al.

13. —claiming to represent the "Light," i.e. a higher spiritual

power, even though the literal translation of the name Lucifer can be "Light Bearer."

14. Neither set of entities ever occupied human bodies of their own.

15. Either set of entities can or could have been "abducted" or "possessed." Without going into great detail, it is convenient to think of the possibilities like this: Demons, or fallen angels, are said to have fallen from grace, even though they were originally created by God. In effect, they may have been influenced, even possessed and/or abducted, by Lucifer at the time of the Great Rebellion in Heaven. ETs (generically meant here to encompass UFO-related entities) are vulnerable to possession and abduction, as well.

16. Both sets or subsets of these entities may have volunteered to interact with humans in these ways.

17. Dr. Baldwin mentions the similarity of the "little demons" to stinging insects. Many UFO percipients report interactions with UFO occupants resembling insects.

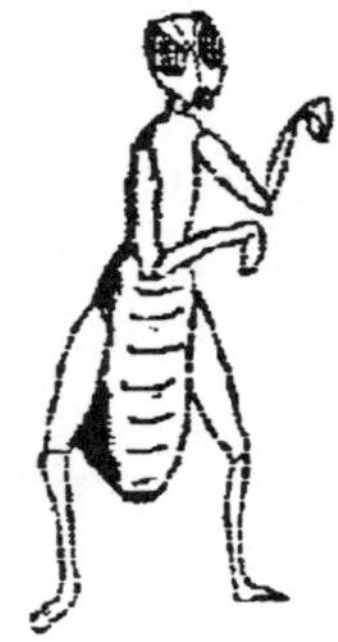

Left: "St. Anthony Fighting the Devil With the Cross." (After Salvator Rosa)—from *The History of the Devil*. **Right:** A composite drawing of a UFO-related "Mantis Being," as reported by many percipients.

18. Worldwide, many government, military and industrial leaders (in addition to the general population) can act in many ways identical to these entities because of the relatively high level of possession or influence the leaders have been subjected to by these entities.

19. —performing their tasks in a highly compartmented fashion, much like our intelligence agencies—and are subjected to a "need to know" protocol that protects the higher echelons and the knowledge base of their organizations from close scrutiny.

20. —able to create robot-like minions capable of performing physical tasks.

21. Possessed ETs have reported through percipients that they have performed similar abductions/tasks on other planets.

22. —emulating voices in the percipients' minds.

23. Many credible researchers see a direct connection between

the so-called UFO phenomenon and black magic. (Keel, Pacheco and Blann, Wilson, et al.)

24. —convincing percipients that they are special "chosen ones," and often promise rewards for cooperation and implementation of the entities' agenda.

25. —trying to hybridize corporeal bodies of their own through genetic and soul level manipulation of human donors.

26. —inducing the dream state, where coded and/or occult (i.e. "hidden") information is often implanted in the percipient's mind for later retrieval or implementation of a designated action.

27. —attempting to dissuade a percipient from using free will, or to exercise that use toward ways that would benefit the entities; both sets of entities also at times appear to outright disregard a percipient's free will.

28. These things the entities are capable of doing, so too, if even in lesser degree, are their minions/victims.

29. —displaying high degrees of familiarity with and command of exotic technology. They also seem capable of influencing humans to develop and utilize technologies considered to be exotic or unique. These latter technologies often owe their genesis to areas having to do with human conflict / destruction.

Clearly, if there are such things as "aliens" and "demons," then they surely have a lot in common, at least as their actions are reported by percipients. Polls consistently suggest that a vast majority of people don't believe in demons, while an even larger majority do believe in angels. It would seem each set of entities is quite adroit at marketing, the angels for helping us to believe in them, and the demons for persuading us not to believe in them!

Belief in ETs undulates with the general population at between 35-50%, depending on the poll you check.

Chapter Four

The Prophets

The point of this discussion thus far, regardless of any particular religious or cultural background, is that whatever these energies represent, they are identified repeatedly throughout history. It used to be that societies had little problem in accepting the seeming dualistic nature of our existence thanks in large part to these non-human intelligences. It seems to be a little more problematic in today's world, as societies readily grasp beliefs in ecology-sensitive huggy aliens and kindly angels without considering the possibility that other less benevolent beings or "intelligence complexes" may also exist.

Part of the problem when it comes to UFOs and associated belief systems is that no mainstream institution or profession cares to put serious research to the subject of UFOs and related phenomena. Science, for the most part, ignores or debunks the subject (namely because there are no funding sources to pay it for investigating the phenomenon), while most mainstream organized religions scorn it. (And as we all know, a belief system without either science or religion behind it is mere philosophy.)

And yet, more and more would-be "UFO prophets" insist on wailing their siren songs across the vast oceans of public opinion, with the result, whether intentionally or not, of potentially luring many more unprepared cosmic sailors onto the rocks.

UFOs, Ecological Disaster

Here are a few examples of how belief systems link with UFOs, the ecology of our planet, and prophecies of ecological disaster.

Reading back over Whitley Strieber's list of books, *Secret School* being his latest, is like seeing how a belief system starts innocently enough (his 1987 best-selling *Communion* did break new ground in the UFO abduction scenario), and then begins to blossom from the perspective of a reporter of

these experiences, to then that as an interpreter of and proponent for "revealed truth" in a few sequels, and finally to the point of being a prophet of truth. He fills the end of *Secret School* with a number of prophecies, many of them dubious and certainly not unique, such things as ecological disaster, ETs saving us from ourselves, etc. If some of his darker predictions come true, there won't be many of us left to pass an opinion on his veracity, however.

Another book in particular, *Ecopsychology: Restoring The Earth, Healing The Mind,*[1] deserves special notice. The back cover of the book lays out its theme: "*Ecopsychology* marks the coming together of leading-edge psychologists and ecologists to redefine sanity on a personal and planetary scale." I don't know about you, but I find it somewhat disconcerting, if not downright "oxymoronic," or at the least amazingly arrogant that a handful of psychologists and ecologists would consider themselves capable of defining sane. Anyway, the book is noteworthy for a study of UFOs because it features an essay originally entitled "Inventing a Psychology of Our Relationship to the Earth."

That essay was written by environmental activist, Harvard psychiatrist, and ***UFO author*** John Mack, M.D., whose 1994 book *Abduction* outlined his interpretation of the stories of many people who sought his psychiatric guidance following their perceived encounters with and abductions by UFO occupants. Not surprisingly, one of Mack's prime observations of his clients' stories is that aliens are here with the dual purpose of "changing human consciousness to prevent the destruction of the earth's life, and a joining of two species for the creation of a new evolutionary form." If you don't agree with Mack's opinion, he has a special term for you, which he reportedly used in a speech overseas a few years ago. "Consciousness challenged," he calls you.

Now, to somehow unite his beliefs of the alien need for hybridizing our species out of existence (genetic level "ethnic cleansing" I guess you could call it) while also getting us to appreciate our planetary sacrificial genocide in the name of saving Mother Gaia* required Mack's broad interpretation of his clients'

experiences. In doing so, he somehow had to elevate his beliefs to heights at least commensurate to current standards of religious dogma or at least of political expediency, for if one is attempting to invent a new psychology and a new definition of sanity, it will need to supplant or at least to influence spirituality, and it will be required to follow a political course, as a means by which to broadly implement its goals. Here's how he is trying to do that.

First, and I must stress that this is my interpretation, he says the old way of looking at things, the duality of our existence, that old notion of an eternal battle between good and evil, despite the fact that it forms the basis of most of the earth's religious beliefs, must be ignored. In its place will come a new dualism: the promotion of a concept of an applied psychology which will "reanimate" nature in a spiritual sense, and of an aggressive philosophy which will convince us to rely on a singularity of perception, not of experience.

In practice, then, Dr. Mack gives us a workable Gaia hypothesis with humans as guilty interlopers upon the Earth, and where aliens are perhaps intermediaries between us and God, representing the true cosmology of our existence. Even though the aliens sometimes abduct people, sometimes subject them to hideous experiments without anesthesia, the ETs are potentially still to be considered "closer than we are to God or the source of being," Mack writes. Thus, the nightmarish and painful experiences abductees suffer are, in fact, merely altered perceptions of what is truly a benevolent reality expressed by a higher intelligence through ecology sensitive alien beings who are perhaps punishing human "intruders."

This may be the ultimate demonstration of the term "tough love."

As humans, it's either Mother Gaia that is attempting the shrug us off the planet, or it's God's intermediaries who are attempting to do it, Mack implies. Either way, we're guilty and we're going to pay.

One presumes, of course, in the meantime before we are finally done away with as a species, that we will be expected to seek ministrations from the eco-shrink-shaman-priests who will administer some as yet undefined combination of eco-scientific/spiritual/psycho-pharmacological modality to help us conform to the new definition of sanity while also accepting our doom with aplomb—all reimbursable, of course with the right insurance plan.)

See if this sounds familiar:

> "This planet is about to be recycled, refurbished, started over. That doesn't mean it's going to be destroyed, it doesn't mean it's the end of the world. But it does mean that it is going to be spaded under."

Is this a quote from Whitley Strieber, the high profile UFO prophet of doom, or from John Mack, the guy who writes in *Ecopsychology* about the necessity of inventing a psychology that is more earth friendly, and who writes in *Abduction* about the total demise of our species? Or is it from Marshall Applewhite, the Heaven's Gate leader? Here's a clue: it's from the guy whose consciousness he believed would lift off with the aliens on March 26, 1997.

It does, indeed, seem quite difficult at times to tell these mens' writings apart. Could they all have been in contact with the same space aliens who carried messages of doom and ecological despair? Maybe. Or could they all have been infected with an information virus, the sort mentioned earlier? Maybe. Or could they all simply be suffering from the same general fantasy? Maybe. Or could they have been subjected to a form of mind control from whatever source? Maybe. Or, finally, could they all be consciously trying to persuade the general population of something? Perhaps. And if so, why?

Questions, questions, questions. My stock in trade as a journalist.

Anyway, these three previously mentioned men are only the tip of an iceberg of a horde of such UFO prophets. Let's look at one more, then move on.

NON-NEWS FLASH!

Here's a non-news flash for you: We are in contact with Martians! And they're here! The ETs are here to mop up the ecological destruction humans have caused, and to breed a new human with less capacity to do harm! So this guy has designated himself a diplomat to the ETs! Sound familiar? Is this Whit Strieber or John Mack again? No, and it isn't a replay of a 1930's radio broadcast, or any other kind of admitted science fiction. It is the published finding of a Ph.D. associate professor of political science

at Emory University. Such is the state of Emory's poly-sci department!

Anyway, this associate professor, Dr. Courtney Brown, wrote a book, *Cosmic Voyage*, which relates his supposed contact with Martians and other sorts of ETs and even with Jesus using remote viewing techniques taught him by a former military remote viewer, Maj. Ed Dames. All the beings Brown claimed to talk to, including the big Guy, spoke back, he says.

Brown, who in addition to his job at Emory is now reportedly moonlighting as a remote viewing instructor for those able to afford his hefty fee, received hearty endorsements on the back cover of his book by none other than BOTH Whitley Strieber and John Mack. Small world.

If any of what Brown says is true is not for us to decide, though I find it a bit irritating that this guy would appoint himself as a sort of ambassador to the stars without first letting the rest of us have a vote on it.

While Brown, Strieber and others attempt to position themselves as unelected, unappointed diplomats to the stars or prophets of UFO revealed truth, there are many people with a very high level of incredulity standing in their way. You will find many of them present in this book.

Nonetheless, some people do continue to be vulnerable to such toxic beliefs.

If statistics are accurate, approximately 85 people ***a day*** kill themselves in the United States.[2] They do so for a wide variety of reasons. Assuredly, they take their own lives because of certain beliefs they hold. The 39 people associated with Heaven's Gate who committed suicide at the mansion in Rancho Sante Fe held very firm beliefs about UFOs.

The major media in this country, woefully ignorant of the UFO phenomenon and all of its associated offshoots, have fallen prey to the sensational side of the story without fully analyzing the broader aspects of it and of the belief systems that it represents.

While the senseless death of 39 people—many of them at the height of their human capacity for creativity and productivity—is a testament to the tragedy of a warped belief system, one of the central but largely overlooked factors involved in the Heaven's Gate mass suicide is a question of the origin of the belief system that led these people to kill themselves. During the week immediately following the suicides, many newspapers began listing the usual litany of psychological problems said to be exhibited by the group's leaders, Marshall Applewhite, a man with a long history of cult-like behaviors, and Bonnie Lu Nettles. (As an aside, it was reported in *USA Today* and other publications that Applewhite was a former psychiatric patient, though no publication pointed out that psychiatry had failed in the end to keep this man from claiming his own life while talking 38 others into joining his barbiturate and alcohol- induced permanent sleep.) But I have yet to see any major media begin to examine a broader spectrum of possible causes of the Heaven's Gate tragedy.

And that takes us back to the "Matrix of UFO Beliefs" we examined a while ago, and then through the partial list of "UFO prophets" currently making the rounds and making a lot of money. That these guys are doing this is one thing, but why they're doing it is another. A sense of (or a real) mission? A real identifiable belief system? Money? I don't know. Whatever the case, they are having some impact on the mass consciousness.

(*referring back to the 1972 "Gaia Hypothesis" as proposed by the English biochemist James Lovelock)

(1. *Ecopsychology: Restoring The Earth, Healing The Mind,* 1995, Theodore Roszak (ed.), Sierra Club Books, San Francisco, CA)

(2. *The World Almanac and Book of Facts, 1997*, World Almanac Books, New Jersey)

Chapter Five

The Grassroots: Highlights And Discussions

So far this briefing has presented the UFO phenomenon mostly from the perspective of various researchers, but it has not yet highlighted the percipients' viewpoint. This chapter will quickly highlight grassroots reports.

Below: A series of two humorous but very insightful paintings by a percipient who succinctly captures the changeable nature of society's belief structure.

On The Wings of

IM137

IM153

IM169

IM171

Key to the Symbols on These Two Pages

From ancient Sumerians to modern Americans, people throughout time have recorded their encounters with winged creatures. Some researchers choose to attribute such run-ins to mythology, while others say the contact is the result of alien visitations, manifestations of spirits, collective fantasy, etc. **Clockwise**, from upper left: **IM137,** a sketch of "Mothman," a figure spotted by hundreds of Point Pleasant, WV, residents in the 1960's, from the cover of John Keel's *Mothman Prophecies*; **IM153**, one representation of Horus, Egyptian god, from *The 12th Planet* by Zecharia Sitchin; **IM169**, "Lamussa," the Assyrian mythological character representing "The Vigilance," from *Symbols, Signs and Signets* by Ernst Lehner; **IM171**, the Occidental "Griffin (16th Century), ibid; **IM49** Amerindian "Piasa Birdman" from *People of the Web* by G. Little; **IM170**, the

(Or, A Bird

IM136

IM160

IM167

IM150

Mythological Perception

IM49

IM170

IM172A

IM172

IM157

IM173

"Ba," Egyptian symbol for the soul, from *Symbols, Signs and Signets*; **IM172A**, 16th Century Occidental symbol, "The Harpy," ibid; **IM172**, 16th Century Occidental symbol, "The Merman," ibid; **IM157**, Oannes, Babylonian god of science and letters, ibid; **IM173**, 18th Century Occidental symbol, "The Hippogryph," ibid; **IM154A**, Babylonian "Winged Guard of the Symbolic Tree," IM154, "Marduc," the Babylonian symbol for "The Creator," ibid; **IM158**, Incan (Peruvian) "God of the Air," ibid; **IM150**, battle between Zeus and Typhon, *The 12th Planet* by Zecharia Sitchin; **IM167**, "Abraxas," a Gnostic gem from Chalres W. King's *The Gnostics and Their Remains*, excerpted from *Symbols, Signs and Signets* by Ernst Lehner; **IM160**, Vedic/Hindu God, "Maja, the Allmother," ibid; **IM136**, the "Jersey Devil," as "humorously depicted in newspapers in 1909," from *People of the Web* by Gregory Little.

In The Hand...)

IM158

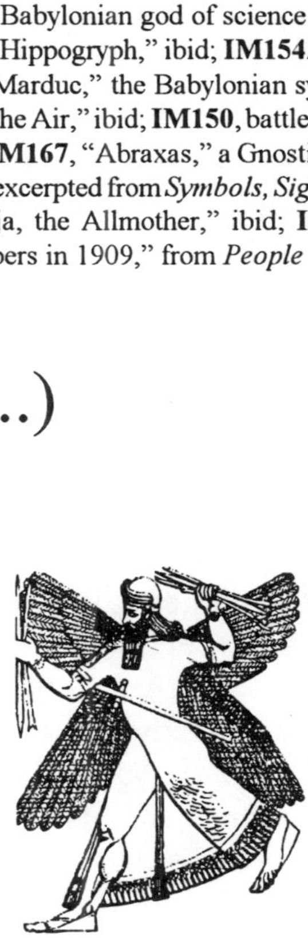

IM154

IM154A

The Grave Creek Stone as a Rock of Ages

A STONE'S THROW TO THE PAST

The core of UFO study, whether it's art in words or pictures, lies in the field's ability to pull you into areas you think totally unrelated to it, and, like the classic childrens' film, *The Never Ending Story*, reward your search with paradox and intrigue.

Consider, for example, a recent serendipitous foray into an area I thought had little to do with UFOs.

In his book, *People of the Web*, Dr. Gregory Little theorizes UFO's as necessary archetypal spiritual manifestations (similar to Blessed Virgin Mary sightings, Amerindian Piasa bird and Mothman appearances, etc.) that are defined by the experiencer, and are the result of the spirits' insistence on interacting with ofttimes ignoble, provincial man. To demonstrate his point he, like John Keel and others, establishes a compelling link between the UFO phenomenon and Amerindian burial mounds.

Figure 1: A scale drawing of the Grave Creek Stone, originally discovered in 1838. Scanned from *West Virginia: Yesterday and*

Background

The Grave Creek Mound, located in the appropriately named *Moundsville*, WV, is the largest conical mound in the U.S., and is believed to have measured about 65' high with a base diameter of 240' at the time of its completion in about 200 B.C. by members of the Adena Culture.[1]

In 1838, Abelard Tomlinson, who owned the property where the sacred site is located, tunneled into the mound with a group of friends, and in early June tore through a wall of logs and entered into a tomb which held two skeletons and various artifacts. Later, the group found another tomb located several feet above the previous one, and along with two additional skeletons and many ornaments, they reportedly discovered a 3/8" thick sandstone tablet measuring about 2" X 1 1/2" that was "inscribed with curious, unrecognizable characters or symbols."[2] (See Figure 1)

The current whereabouts of the stone are unknown, last being seen around the turn of the century when an Ohioan reportedly paid 50-cents for it at a junk sale.

Since the time of its discovery and subsequent disappearance, the stone's purported authenticity has spurred raging debates among archaeologists and others. Additionally, various scholars throughout the world have attempted to decipher the mysterious symbology, often with dubious results, and have thus contributed mightily to the obfuscation surrounding the tablet.

Perhaps parodying these attempts, a Moundsville resident offered the following translation in 1907: "United States of Egypt, built by States of Western Union."[3]

Regardless of these interpretations and the furor over the stone's authenticity, the symbols (if even dating back no further than the early 1830s) and letters do offer some interesting parallels to those recognized as being associated with UFOlogy. (See Figure 2)

Figure 2: The "Grave Creek Stone" symbols compared to others used at various times in differing cultures. See key next two pages.

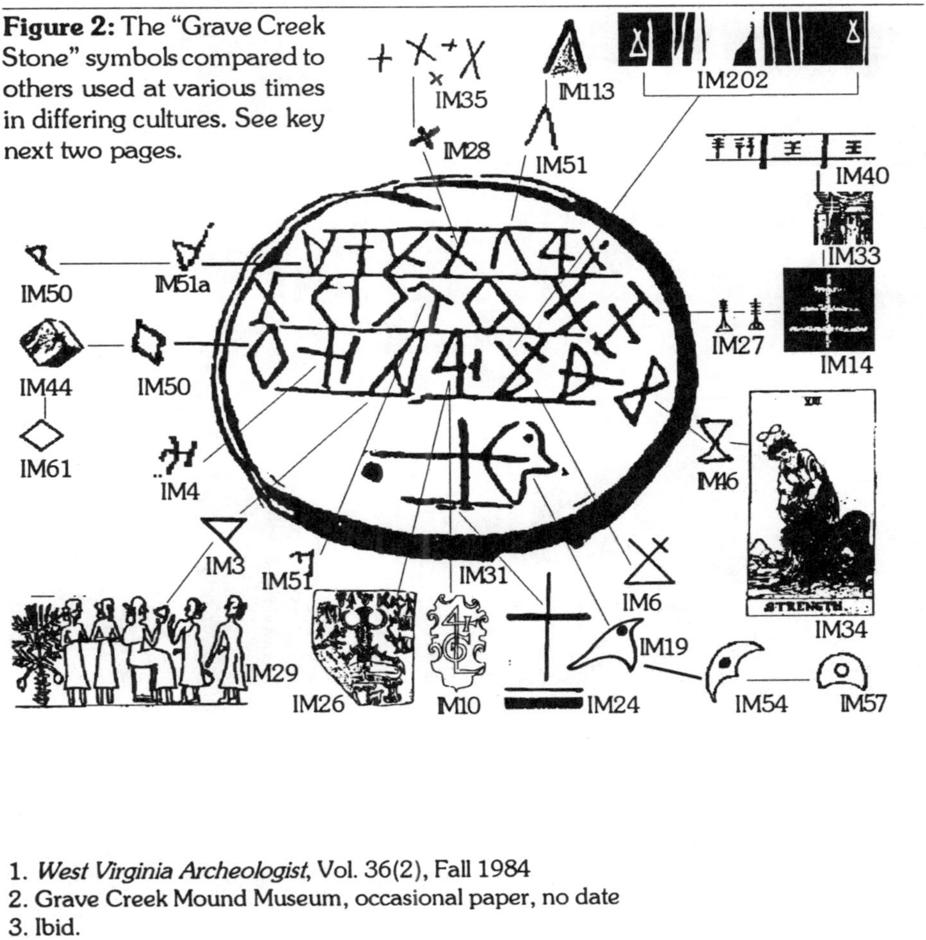

1. *West Virginia Archeologist*, Vol. 36(2), Fall 1984
2. Grave Creek Mound Museum, occasional paper, no date
3. Ibid.

Key To The Stone Symbols

IM3: Alchemy symbol for "the crucible." *Source:* ***Symbols, Signs & Signets*** *by Ernst Lehner*

IM4: One symbol from an alphabet and pronunciation guide said to have been given to a New York abductee in 1955. *Source:* ***An Alien Harvest*** *by Linda Moulton Howe*

IM6: Roman stonemason mark. Source: ***Symbols, Signs & Signets*** *by Ernst Lehner*

IM202: The mark on two of these ET's suits bears a resemblance to one such symbol found on the stone. Source: ***Matrix III,*** *by Valdamar Valerian (illustrator unknown)*

IM10: Circa 1593 French watermark. Source: ***Symbols, Signs & Signets*** *by Ernst Lehner*

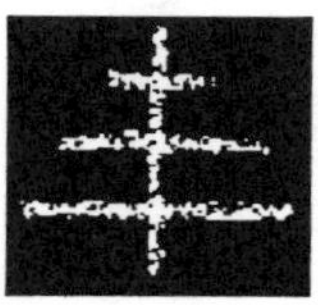

IM14: American hobo sign for "officer." Source: ***Symbols, Signs & Signets*** *by Ernst Lehner*

IM19: A symbol for, "Darkened earth will spin in different directions," psychically received by multiple abductee Mary M. Wunder in 1991. *Source:* ***A Message From the Stars****, by Wunder.*

IM24: A symbol for, "God is strong," psychically received by multiple abductee Mary M. Wunder in 1991. *Source:* ***A Message From the Stars****, by Wunder.*

IM26: The numeral 4, from a Sumerian cylinder drawing, circa 3,200 B.C. *Source:* ***The 12th Planet*** *by Zecharia Sitchin*

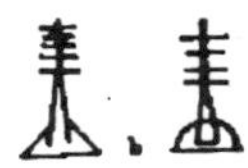

IM27: Antennae from a Sumerian cylinder drawing, circa 3,200 B.C. *Source:* ***The 12th Planet*** *by Zecharia Sitchin*

IM28: Symbols from a Sumerian cylinder drawing, circa 3,200 B.C. *Source:* ***The 12th Planet*** *by Zecharia Sitchin*

IM29: From a Sumerian cylinder drawing, circa 3,200 B.C. *Source:* ***The 12th Planet*** *by Zecharia Sitchin*

IM33: The Papal Cross, as depicted on "The Hierophant" Tarot card. *Source:* ***Intangible Evidence****, by Bernard Gittelson*

IM34: The lemniscate above the woman's head on this Tarot card is also a universal sign for infinity. *Gittelson*

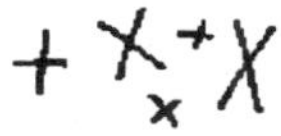

IM35: Special markings relied on by the palmist and that signify "sudden or drastic change that may be positive or negative." *Source: **Intangible Evidence**, by Bernard Gittelson*

IM40: Sumerian alphabet characters that were destined to become the letter X in English. *Source: **The 12th Planet** by Zecharia Sitchin*

IM44: One of a list of "Hard Objects" report-edto have been spotted by UFO watchers. *Source: **The Other**, by Brad Steiger*

IM46: One of the many symbols Jesse Marcel Jr. drew in hypnotic trance while recalling his examination of an I-beam that his father had in his possession following the alleged crash of a disk in Roswell, New Mexico in 1947. *Source: **UFO Crash at Roswell**, by Kevin D. Randle and Donald R. Schmitt.*

IM50: Abduction experiences, as reported and drawn by a Nebraska man. Many of the symbols appearing on the tee-pee, including two in common with the Grave Creek Stone, are familiar to UFOlogists. *Source: R. G. Teets*

IM51: Symbols reportedly seen by UFOlogist Sean David Morton as he awoke from sleeping in the coffin of Cheops. *Source: **The Millennium Factor**, by Sean David Morton.*

IM54: The reported shape of a flying saucer included in a 1958 wall poster. *Source: "Flying Saucers" poster, ©1958 by Fred Keziah.*

IM57: The reported shape of a flying saucer included in a 1958 wall poster. *Source: "Flying Saucers" poster, ©1958 by Fred Keziah.*

IM61: The reported shape of a flying saucer included in a 1958 wall poster. *Source: "Flying Saucers" poster, ©1958 by Fred Keziah.*

IM113: 1992 sketch by abductee Mary M. Wunder of an alien with insignia. Source: **A Message From the Stars**, by Mary M. Wunder

Notes

Relative to IM46 above:

An obscure book by S. T. Wiley, *The History of Preston County* (West Virginia), published in 1883, offers the following intriguing observation of an artifact uncovered in 1834 from an Amerindian burial mound located approximately 100 miles from the Grave Creek Mound in rural Preston County:

> ***"...found in it...a very peculiar stone relic in the shape of an hour-glass, which was mechanically constructed, neatly dressed, and capable of being used for the purpose of recording time."***

Left: a creature spotted by a group of teenagers on a camping trip near a small town in West Virginia during a UFO flap.

Right: Here's a drawing of a famous September, 1952 sighting of the so-called Flatwoods Green Monster, a creature said by eyewitnesses to have emerged from a crashed vehicle. A total of three "constructions" were reportedly seen flying then crashing in or near the same West Virginia area that day. This event occurred only a few months after the widely reported July, 1952 UFO flap in Washington, D.C., witnessed by hundreds, where crafts were said to have encircled the city and to have even broken the no-fly zone over the White House.

Left: These alien creatures were drawn by a male multiple abductee.

Right: A Nebraska male multiple abductee drew this image of one abduction experience from the 1950s, this time involving an entire crowd of residents of Lincoln, Nebraska.

Above: The same Nebraska man depicted this personal abduction scene from the late 1940s.

Left: Here's one of the latest cryptozoological creatures to make the scene, the so-called Chupacabras or "goat sucker" that originated in Puerto Rico and then spread to parts of South and North America. (With permission of the *San Juan Star*)

GUYS WITH BIG EYES

While this cast of characters may not be your ideal neighbor-next-door types (though many UFOlogists claim that to be the case, including author Whitley Strieber, whose almond-eyed ET stared at us from over 1-million copies of his best-selling book), these guys have been portrayed by their artists as this era's basic ET-book stock portraiture. Note the conformity of salient details, the standards for which, some say, were set by Strieber's fabulously successful book and cover. **Clockwise**, from top left: **IM197** is taken from the cover of *A Message From The Stars* by Mary M. Wunder. **IM196** features the cover of *The Other* by Brad Steiger. **IM220,** labelled "Extra-Systemics from Reticulum," was taken from *Matrix* by Valdamar Valerian (no artist mentioned). **IM218** appeared amidst an article about the allegedly secret "Dulce Papers," ibid. **IM187** is, according to Steiger's *The Other*, artist Hal Crawford's conception of the "Alpha Form Humanoid," which he "based on dozens of eyewitness accounts." **IM204** offers conspiracy lovers with a euphoric titillation in the form of military guys meeting big eyes, from *Matrix III* by Valdamar Valerian (the author's name is believed to be a pseudonym). **IM194** is an artist's conception of the 1965 French connection between Maurice Masse and beam-shooting guys. **IM219** is Charles Johnson's 1988 depiction of typical "gray" guys used to illustrate author George Andrews' article entitled, "A Tentative Taxonomy of Extra-Terrestrial Humanoids," included in *Matrix* by the pseudonym-hungry Valdamar Valerian.

IM197

IM196

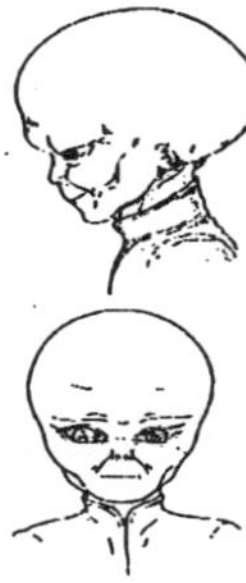

IM219

IM220

IM194

IM204

IM187

IM218

Beauty... and the Beasts

IM210

IM190

IM191

IM192

Well, look at it this way: Would there be any Mattell without Barbie and Ken? UFOlogy does have its Charming Couples (but a startling absense of most any but Caucasian beauties and hunks), like the pair above, and its Odd Couples, like the pair of scarry guys flanking these words. In any case, and given the respective designations of three of these characters by Brad Steiger, one is tempted to lump them as the strangest fraternity in existence: the Beta-Delta-Gamma guys. **IM190**, above left, is labelled the "Beta Humanoid" Space Brother (obviously a sibling of the angelic Space Sister featured on the next page) in *The Other* by Brad Steiger. **IM210** is a popular seller (particularly if you're into snake eyes) at UFO conventions in the form of an 11" X 14" mountable black and white wall poster, with the artist's signature, *B. Curnock*. ($14.95 market price in 1995), *with B. Curnock's permission*. **IM192** (right) is considered by Steiger to be a "Delta-Form Humanoid capable of assuming any shape or size." (Compare to the Mothman illustration on Page 45). **IM191** is the Gamma-Form (Bigfoot) guy, Steiger says. Numerous independent eyewitnesses will swear the Steiger creatures to be "real."

Above: Stylized beings and repeated abduction experiences reportedly never "consciously" recalled except late at night when the percipient "feels an urge to paint." The same female, Suzie B., produced the renditions on the following two pages...

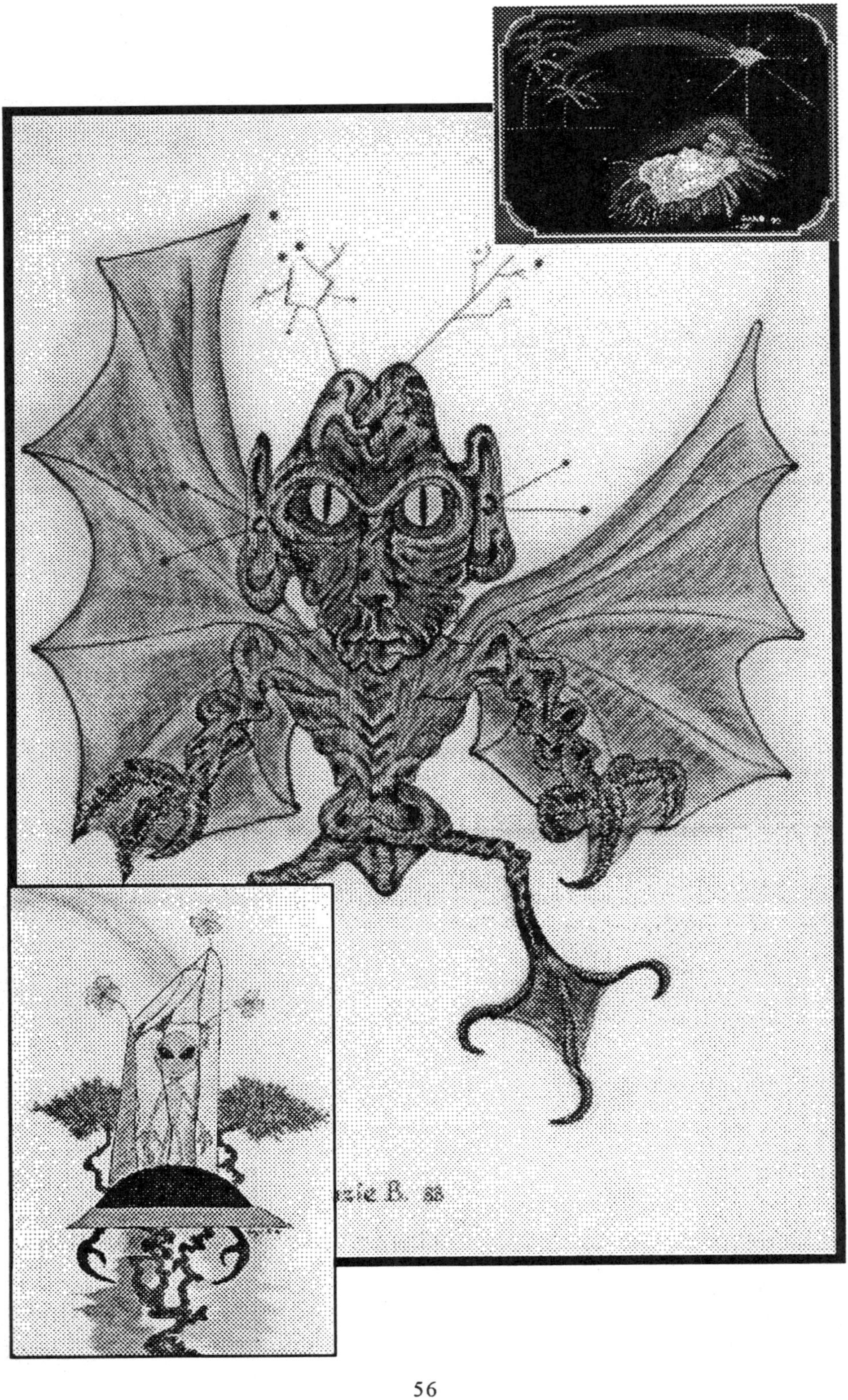

Beings depicted on the Heaven's Gate web page.

Crafts

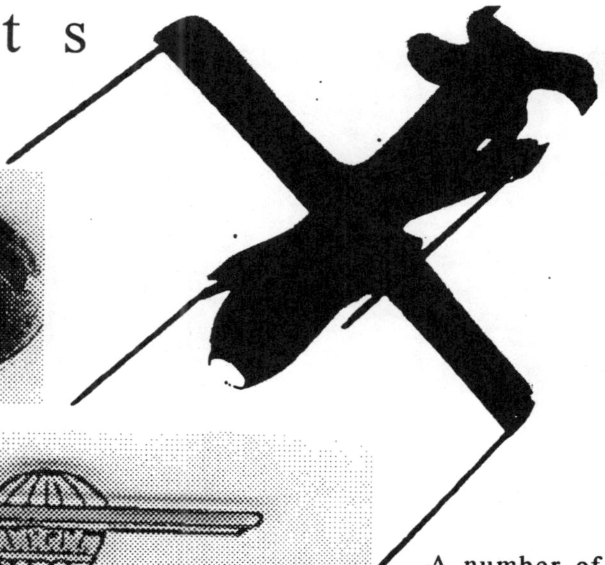

A number of different "crafts" are depicted here, all reportedly built by human hands. The models at left are said to have been German World War II era vehicles, while the two at the top are more modern remote piloted crafts developed in North America.

Another way that this phenomenon can take a person is on a ride of educational weirdness, as researcher Robyn Andrews Quail contends she's seen demonstrated in people whose IQ's shoot up immediately after a close encounter. She details some scenarios in a booklet, *Prodigies: Extraterrestrial Telepathic Intelligence Phenomenon.* John Travolta did a movie not long ago which sort of highlighted this, entitled "Phenomenon."

UFOs outrank Social Security

Above: A newspaper headline declares that among a younger age group polled, more believed in UFOs than in the long term viability of the nation's Social Security system.

DISCUSSION

Knock, knock! Who's There?

By Dick Farley

Let us assume for the moment—when a counselor, hypnotherapist or otherwise, encounters a client who believes or comes to believe he or she has experienced what is popularly termed a "UFO encounter" or an "alien abduction"—that CONTACT is being made with another intelligence. The question before us is, "Whose?" Client's? E.T.? Angels? Demons? Ego? Id? Spirits? God? Uh, oh.

Consequently, the challenge for the clinician or counselor, in addition to the ostensible purpose of any client-counselor encounter (i.e., to help the client understand, relax into and perhaps even to integrate their experience), might then additionally include representing Earth culture in a diplomatic exchange taking place somewhere between the conscious mind of the percipient and the interstitial place of residence of the purported "other." At least, such is implied in various of popular beliefs.

How many of us are prepared, at the droop of an eyelid, to become "inter-dimensional diplomats," charged not only with representing the best interests and psychological balances of a client "UFO percipient," but also (in keeping with "alien intelligence" scenarios) those of *homo sapiens* at large?

This brief essay, in the context of this book, encourages that we put aside most of the distortions, denials and disinformation inherent in this field currently, to encourage our reader-practitioners to inquire of purported "UFO knock-knocks" with an open minded, "Who's there?" ("Why?" Later!)

Counseling within what is popularly termed the "UFO / alien abduction" paradigm sadly has taken on some of the coloration of those unfortunately overly popular television solicitations for high-priced psychic-advisor services: "All it takes is a telephone and an open mind." Without the phone.

Criticisms of "UFO abduction" regressions, emanating both from the field's outside skeptics and from within it among practitioners of competing "schools," legitimately center on the potentials for "counselor bias" and identifiable tendencies for at least some practitioners to "lead their witness."

What I am suggesting for consideration here is: What if we all were to pay a bit less attention to the nature and purported genesis of the "visiting others" our percipient-clients are describing, so as to pay closer attention to the information clients believe they are drawing from their experiences, while better assessing and considering the impact of such perceived information on clients' lives?

The previously described *Matrix of UFO Beliefs* is organized into variants of "What people may believe about UFOs." I designed it as an analytical tool to aid in a political decision (in this case, by the President of the United States in a context of his being approached for "UFO declassification"), of: whether, how or how much (if any) currently classified UFO information ought to be released.

The *Matrix* was not intended as an instrument of persuasion for our President and his senior aides about whether to let purported government UFO secrets "out of the bag," as it were. My assumption was and remains that our Presidents do know many secrets, including about things we citizens do not even suspect are real let alone are being withheld from consensus reality.

Rather, the *Matrix* was (and is) a suggested guide for how the President and his aides might go about deciding whether and to what degree to release any such data, considering the potential psychological and cultural impacts on various sectors of the U.S. and planetary populace.

One of the underlying presumptions of the "UFO Declassification Initiative" then being advanced to the White House, and to which the *Matrix* was lent for background support, was the frightening possibility that all Presidents might not be receiving all of the relevant briefing materials in terms of "UFOs" and "alien abductions," as these are now being most broadly defined.

Putting daunting Constitutional ramifications aside if such "selective briefings" of our Commander in Chief and most senior elected official have indeed been the case, in terms of national agenda and psychiatric health of our culture any Presidential decision about "UFO declassification" impacts us intensely with consequences these disclosures have on the U. S. citizenry and our "mental health."

Thus, what "experiencers" of purported UFO and "alien abduction" perceptions recall about any such source phenomena have, from the political and cultural perspectives, potential importance to public officials charged with assessing "whether and what and how" to disclose, if indeed there is "anything there." Without more clinical rigor and balanced analysis, it's difficult to learn anything.

Which brings us to potential definitions of "anything." And these depend on your own perspective.

If you are the United States Air Force, you are once again attempting unconvincingly to explain away public sightings and "encounters" with alleged "crashed flying saucer wreckage" and "alien bodies" around New Mexico defense research installations

50 years ago as "reconnaissance balloon" experiments and "crash-test dummies" dropped from high altitudes for parachute testing.

And in keeping with no doubt legitimate protection of undisclosed secrets like "stealth" aircraft technology and other bizarre exotica of aeronautical types, you'd want to allow sufficient lingering uncertainty after any "Roswell UFO disclosures" so that other, potentially unfriendly air forces don't believe a word of it and remain convinced you've got something REALLY BIG yet hiding.

If you were an aging, retired military or intelligence officer, who had helped to perpetrate a Cold War-era aeronautical hoax against the Soviet Union or other political targets, would you want to be the focal point of cultural wrath because your "UFO hoax" worked so well it's become a religion?

Perhaps this is the position of retired U. S. Army Colonel Philip J. Corso, who in a recent (1997) book, *The Day After Roswell: A Former Pentagon Official Reveals the U. S. Government's Shocking UFO Cover-Up,* contended that he (Corso) was part of a secret Pentagon effort taking apart various "alien artifacts." Allegedly recovered in 1947's "crashed flying saucer" at Roswell, NM, these "alien gadgets," Colonel Corso asks readers to believe, were "reverse engineered" by some of America's largest research institutions and scientific firms, stimulating breakthroughs in solid-state computer chip technology, electro-magnetics, materials sciences and communications.

Fine as far as it goes, notwithstanding his "extra-terrestrial spin." Apparently unforeseen by Colonel Corso and his ultra-conservative allies in what are demonstrable if obtuse "UFOs-or-not" dialogues among defense and disarmament policy wonks, was the near simultaneous publication of a timely UFO-disclosures article in the odd venue of *Popular Mechanics* magazine. This article (August, 1997) bought into the "crashed aerial vehicle" scenario, sure enough. But the "alien" components of the "UFO crash" were attributed to more likely scenarios involving post-World War II testings of captured German and Japanese technologies, among our government's most embarrassing secrets.

So it's understandable why Colonel Corso and others in government now or by now retired might prefer to cash in on the current "UFO rage," rather than face civil rage after a Presidential release of information about past roles in Project Paperclip, which merged ex-Nazi scientists, psychiatrists and spies (and exotic technology) into the American fold to work against Soviet global hegemony.

If you are the U. S. Central Intelligence Agency, you've known for half a century that your various counterintelligence and "mind-bendings" targeted at enemy personnel and populations had required you to fool your own American citizens along the way (and not a few elected officials, too). What might be going through your collective institutional mind about your being "outed" by a President?

First would be damage-control, by disclosing your most benign "UFO-related" activities. You will pick ones you might be able to justify sufficiently to pacify at least most civilians and their elected officials, who have been bamboozled through five decades of carefully constructed disinformation.

CIA did precisely that in its rather remarkable "confession" early in 1997, eventually picked up by a *New York Times* science writer and amplified by wire services worldwide. Entitled "CIA's Role In The Study of UFOs, 1947-90" (*Studies In Intelligence, Semiannual Declassified Edition*, No. 1, 1997), CIA's disclosure sends a clear signal to counselors of "UFO experiencers" that, at best, "things are not always what they might seem." At worst, and given previously disclosed CIA (and other agency) abuses of our citizens and those of other nations, there may be evidences of abusive psychiatric experimentation.

Conspiracy minded? Let's say you are among the self-anointed Anglo-American or allied European elites who believe that you run the world (and do indeed regularly manipulate financial and global events sufficiently that a case can be made that you do). Would you not want to be "in the loop" and "ahead of the curve" if some "other intelligence" began to communicate with Earth's citizenry?

Would you care whether such communications originated in the minds of over-stressed humans or were from inhabiting "interstitial spaces" of our emerging quantum reality or the deeper reaches of interstellar space? Not very likely if "somebody" began to communicate with suitably sensitive and open-minded (pun intended) percipients "here on Earth." You as an Earth leader just have to know!

That is apparently what some major financial backers behind

the last decade's run-up to increasing awareness among our planetary public about "UFOs" and "alien abductions" believed to be their mandate. Professional clinical awareness and the information exchanges about these topics and the organizations which either adapted or were created to publicize them have had identifiable backers.

Elderly billionaire industrialist Laurance S. Rockefeller was among the "background UFO funders" with, despite his best efforts, a relatively high public profile. It was Mr. Rockefeller who mustered powerful political and religious personalities to approach President Bill Clinton in 1993 and 1994, about letting go of some of the U. S. secrets pertaining to UFOs. Interestingly, joining the U. S. Air Force and CIA in opposing (and defusing) Rockefeller's efforts were our long-present "UFO investigation" organizations, clearly tied to government through their memberships and leadership.

Another billionaire industrialist, Prince Hans Adam II of Liechtenstein, also a major player in the European Union and environmental-globalist Club of Rome, contributed to several of the crucial "UFO" conferences in the early 1990s, specifically those widely popularizing "alien abductions" as a paradigm for hypno-therapy regression and analysis. Prince Hans Adam also was joined in his sponsorship of the watershed 1992 MIT Abduction Study Conference by Las Vegas entrepreneur Robert Bigelow, who continues funding frontier research efforts into the UFO field.

These are facts about where and how the "UFO therapies" and "alien abductions" paradigms arose. But why, if you were among men promoting these admittedly "leading edge" considerations about human psychology and planetary culture, would you risk your reputation to facilitate such study?

You would be irresponsible to your self-annointed station in life among our "planetary elite" if you did not pay close attention, whether such "experiences" were a result of actual communication from "elsewhere" and "others," or even more so if such perceptions result from a previously undescribed cultural psychosis. And if some "percipients" of UFO encounters are victims of an unknown form of external mind-influencing technology or information virus, investigation would be compulsory!

As is reflected in the *Matrix of UFO Beliefs*, and in the supportive literature and collective human experiences and research on which that analytical tool is based, each of the preceding scenarios and situations has some factual basis and a constituency of believers in the field we broadly call UFOs.

Counselors and therapists should become better able to appreciate this. And to their clients and to a significant cohort of our U. S. and planetary populations, "UFO counselors" in essence appear to be making a FIRST CONTACT with some kind of "unknown others" desiring to influence Earth's consciousness and, in our political realms, our planet's organization, our priorities and our futures.

What even skeptics and "UFO sympathizers" can agree on is this: "Something is going on!" It is in our respective and multi-variant interpretations, driven in no small way by our respective fears and biases and even our own desires, where the essential elements of mutual respect and understanding tend to break down, often times seemingly by "external design." Net result? Paralyzing confusion!

We know that various powerful terrestrial forces, ranging from defense and intelligence community interests of various nations (and undoubtedly transnational entities) to various religions striving to turn their "revealed truths" and theologies into planetary policies, are heavily invested and strongly present in arenas such as: UFOs, alien abductions, planetary ecology and psychiatric manipulation.

What we do not yet know is whether our fellow humans who've come to recall or to believe they have become some part of this unrolling planetary political psychodrama can find sufficiently good and unbiased interventions which will help them cope with whatever may be going on.

Whether whatever "it" is takes place inside their heads and minds, or perhaps comes from outside, what we all can confirm from our collective experiences thus far is that the various "beliefs" which are associated with these phenomena exert powerful influences to the very innermost depths of our psyches and on our cultural perspective and ambition. Counseling therapists who aim at counseling "UFO" percipients will do well to park their own biases and beliefs before asking, "Who's there?"

Chapter Six

Remote Viewing: Warriors Without Armor

(Note: Dr. Hal Puthoff did not respond to a request for an interview. Mr. Dick D'Amato did not respond to a faxed offer for advance information, and could not be located in his office despite repeated calls. Look for more information and, we hope, personal interviews with these two individuals in future editions of The American UFO Newsletter.*)*

Heaven's Gate founders Marshall Applewhite and Bonnie Lu Nettles considered themselves prophets after having been in contact over many years, they said, with non-human intelligences connected with UFOs. Nancy Reagan is said to have regularly consulted an astrologer, and then used the information she obtained to discuss national policy with the President. Hillary Clinton supposedly consulted with the discarnate spirit of Eleanor Roosevelt via a medium. From the earliest times, most kings and rulers have at some time sought advice from soothsayers, scryers and prophets who also claimed to be in touch with such entities. Religions, as well, have relied on prophets to foretell the future and the arrival of renowned leaders, foes and disasters. The ancient Greeks called on their oracles and seers to peek into the future, to speak with the dead or the gods for advice on topics ranging from the most mundane, like shopping trips, to the most important, like war.

And now we know Uncle Sam officially did the same thing over a period exceeding at least two decades, beginning in 1972.

Dressed up in new terms, but still evoking images of smoky fires and sacrificial virgins or drug-laden shamans, the officially sanctioned military/intelligence seers and tarot card readers were casually known as "remote viewers," and although the government now says it is out of the remote viewing business (officially, the government says it axed its interest in the subject during 1994-95), the so-called "process" of RV'ing developed by Uncle Sam with taxpayer funding is now offered for sale to the same taxpayers and general public at any number of locations around the country by former RV'ers and their erstwhile students who say anyone can perform these feats of psychic prowess. Since the process is otherworldly, the price is sky-high, as well, and can range in excess of $1,000. However, given the at best dubious and sometimes silly and ridiculous results reported as true by some of these RV'ers in public forums, one could garner analogous information for $20 from a county fair palm reader.

But one must wonder if the government's new-found distaste for remote viewing, and the sometimes silly results the now public remote viewers espouse isn't perhaps a smoke screen intended to deceive the public into thinking RV'ing is not effective. The government did issue a report of a study conducted by the American Institutes for Research (AIR) on the latter years of the remote viewing program, and to no one's surprise, the report found little use for or reliability of remote viewing as a tool for spying/ intelligence gathering. It's believed, however, that the AIR study was over-staffed with debunkers.

Skeptics of the report, however, including many of the original remote viewers themselves, believe the government did, in fact, find some utility to the remote viewing process, particularly in the early years of the CIA-sponsored research program. To date, no one has suggested publicly that Uncle Sam has continued a covert RV program, though evidence does exist which proves the government's past interest in related areas of mind research and mind control.

Implications: Star Wars and Cat Magic

According to several sources, many of the soldier-scryers involved in the government program also considered themselves part of a futuristically envisioned band of freedom fighters not unlike the Jedi Knights featured in the *Star Wars* films. For sure, and in keeping with the theme, one of their documented tasks during the operational phase of the 20-year remote viewing program was to dowse UFOs. (This last point, once again, points to official government interest in UFOs despite denials from most government / military sources.)

Others in the program used age-old methods of scrying, such as "reading" tarot cards, while a purported documentary on the subject hinted that certain participants relied on protocols identical to black magic and witchcraft in attempting to remote view a target.

As an aside, it is not all that unusual for witchcraft and UFOs to be linked, if even in subtle ways: Best-selling UFO author Whitley Strieber once wrote a front cover endorsement of a book, *Power of the Witch,* by so-called "white witch" Laurie Cabot. Strieber is also quoted as saying that UFOs are about "evocational magic," and that anyone interested in his so-called "UFO" books are encouraged to also read his book *Cat Magic.* In his latest book, *Secret School,* Strieber seems to use such methods to conjure up a number of prophecies.

The Great (Covert) Debate

Depending on one's outlook, these remote viewers and their scientist friends could, indeed, have been considered heroes, as a number of recent books have provided not only intriguing insights into the government's use of these psychics, but of the successful methods by which these warriors provided valuable data to the U. S. command structure. (Author Alex Constantine vehemently argues against this idea, see Chapter 6.) On a larger scale, the government's coordinated and purportedly scientific research and development (beginning in 1972 at Stanford Research Institute) of the remote viewing process, as highlighted in these books, offered fascinating glimpses into human consciousness and brain/mind abilities.

Promoters of remote viewing billed it as a non-lethal means of gathering valuable information which may not otherwise have been accessible. They even envisioned a time when remote viewing could develop an "applied" component which would allow remote influencing of events and outcomes. In its most advanced forms, they said, remote viewing could result in an elite corps of shaman soldiers capable of overpowering enemies on a whole new level—the interstitial field of battle—without firing a shot. So successfully did these proponents make their cases that over time they had enlisted support from some top military and intelligence agency brass and powerful politicians capable of covertly operating and financing such a program.

At its worst, however, the government's remote viewing program, like any covert activity shielded from the American public, held the potential for waste, centralization of power fueled by ego, and possible abuse, this time on a level most basic to human existence—the mind. With the possibility of influencing human minds from a distance, remote viewing held for its detractors the fear of the final ascension of Big Brother—a secret government holding a weapon far more valuable and far more terrifying than the apocalyptic thermonuclear devices once relied on to assure peace through mutually assured destruction. Mind control implemented through remote viewing, they feared, would become the New World Order's ultimate weapon, a tool for assuring peace through mutually assured distraction... a subtle weapon capable of easing shut the lid of a coffin holding the corpus of democracy and of human freedom. (Kings and rulers of old traditionally relied on their own agents provocateur to incite "controllable unrest" in their kingdoms in order to promote factions in the populace who would blame each other—instead of the kings— for their misery. Some say today's American society is manipulated in much the same way, where racial strife, economic stratification and other means are employed to keep us at each other's throats while the rulers continue to unobtrusively accumulate their wealth and power. Thus, "applied" remote viewing—remote influencing—could serve the dual function of keeping tabs on the populace while also pinpointing groups or individuals capable of building weak but highly visible factions within the general population.)

Caught In Between

Thrown into this adamant yet covert maelstrom of debate was a handful of so-called psychics and scientists seeking first to understand the mechanics and perhaps even the metaphysics of psychic abilities, and second to develop the protocols for enhancing those abilities for the purpose of military/intelligence uses. In a sense, these people were explorers following a pock-marked pathway tread for centuries by the shamans and witches of lore and right up through the 20th Century by drug-ingesting would-be gurus in search of spiritual meaning and relevance.

Theirs was not an enviable task, for they had to contend along the way with the ghosts of past and present, from the "Witch of Endor" mentioned in the Bible, through the black "magick" of Aleister Crowley and his ancient predecessors, to the bout of consciousness vs. ego elucidated by Dr. John Lilly in *The Center of the Cyclone*, to the psychedelic drug-induced "ego-death" advocated by Dr. Stanislav Grof in *Beyond the Brain,* to the silly pandering of the drug culture by consciousness/UFO nomads like Terence McKenna.

And while the psychics and scientists were armed with an

awesome array of modern technology and maybe even with impressive psychic abilities, it is doubtful if they were equipped to engage the energies which appeared to wait for them "on the other side." As the internecine shenanigans of the developing remote viewer program unfolded over time, according to various books, it would seem as if these were warriors without armor, gifted soldiers sacrificed to the types of gods whose recreation is the tormenting of humankind and its constructed, combined ego.

Background

The government's so-called "coordinate remote viewing" (CRV) program—whose aim, among others, was to psychically spy on American enemies, to locate missing aircraft and soldiers, and even to dowse UFOs— carried various code names like *Grill Flame, Sun Streak* and later *Stargate,* and reportedly cost approximately $20 million over two decades.

Once called coordinate remote viewing, or CRV'ing, it's now commonly referred to as RV'ing— not to be confused with the type of RV'ing one may do on a camping trip in a recreational vehicle, though "tripping" may be a proper term for these military psychics who spent years in a secret program to spy on Russia while resting somewhat uncomfortably in a special chair at Ft. Meade, Maryland or at Stanford Research Institute (SRI)—and involves a supposed process of accessing information psychically, often employing a form of out-of-body experience. A popular New York psychic named Ingo Swann is said to have joined with some scientists in developing a certain protocol that would aid certain gifted individuals in sharpening their psychic abilities. Of course, and as reported personally to me and to others by one of the RV participants, U.S. military and intelligence communities sought also to use it as an offensive weapon. After all, the theory was that the Russians had been successfully using remote viewing for decades. Rumors had spread for a time that it was a gaggle (herd? bevy? *coven?*) of Russian psychics who had influenced Ronald Reagan into caving into Mikhail Gorbachev and nearly giving away the nuclear farm during the Reykjavik Summit in October, 1986. (Many stories still circulate about British government use of witches during World War II to influence Hitler and Axis leaders to deploy troops in the wrong places during D-Day and in other important battles.)

After the news of RV'ing broke— and break it did, with all

the leading media in the country jumping on the story in 1995 like an RV'er to a target—a plethora of RV'ers published books or otherwise fought for a coveted space in the limelight in order to cash in on their newfound fame. Two supposed viewers, Maj. Ed Dames and Capt. David Morehouse, even founded a company, Psi Tech, which claimed it could RV anything for a price. Some American companies apparently retained Dames' firm, though no one has announced what results were obtained, or what companies participated. (It has been reported that another famous psychic, Uri Geller, the subject of some early experimentation in psi-related stuff at Stanford Research Institute and elsewhere, is now making millions psychically locating oil for tycoons. One RV'er of the early years, Pat Price, left his employment as a remote viewer at SRI to become president of a West Virginia coal company where he reportedly remote viewed for rich coal seams, while also going to work for CIA's RV program, according to the book *Remote Viewers,* reviewed below.)

The Books

A supposed best-seller, *Psychic Warrior: Inside The CIA's Stargate Program,* published in November of 1996, tells the decidedly lop-sided story of one RV'er, an up-and-coming Army officer named David Morehouse. According to his book, a stray bullet during a training exercise hit him in the head (he was wearing a helmet at the time) and left him psychically inclined. He reportedly began experiencing encounters with other-dimensional beings and intelligences, as well as having precognitive dreams and visions, all of which were discouraged by some higher-up brass. He says his abilities were eventually recognized by the then-secret RV program directors, and he was recruited into Stargate and taught the ropes by others in the program. In his book, he claims his own great success in the program, though he traces a litany of self-sacrifices he had to make for his country (like destroying his marriage and family, for instance), and the price he had to pay for trusting the double-dealing government. All the while, he says, he continued to interface with a host of non-human intelligence complexes.

Later, he was reportedly paid an extravagant advance on royalties to write a book along with Ed Dames and another man about RV'ing. The book was never published, though he is said to have leased a Mercedes with his share of the advance. He was later to have received another six figure advance to write *Psychic Warrior*, and is now reportedly the recipient of another huge sum in exchange for the movie rights to the book and a children's television program about superheroes using psychic powers to defeat the bad guys. The book jacket to *Psychic Warrior* says Morehouse is now living in Baltimore, MD, and is apparently writing and lecturing about peace, most recently at the Mikhail Gorbachev Foundation's 1995 State of the World Forum—a warrior tamed.

A Different Light

Another book portrays Morehouse and the Sun Streak/Stargate programs in a totally different light.

Remote Viewers: The Secret History of America's Psychic Spies,[1] which more aptly covers the subject, and which is definitely better and more interestingly written, comes from UFO author and researcher Jim Schnabel. This book takes off the gloves and begins slapping around several of the heretofore secret people behind the scenes of the RV program, including CIA personnel and government military and civilian officials.

This is not to say that Schnabel has written the definitive book about RV'ing. The extraordinary access to details and supposed secrets he exposes in his book certainly suggests this guy was granted access for a purpose. Someone at the top opened the door to Jim and let him find what they wanted him to find.

Nonetheless, it's an extraordinary book that should be required reading for every American citizen.

Schnabel points out the internecine relationships of the major players involved in the RV programs, including spies, military and political leaders and others. In a few deft pages, Schnabel "outs" Morehouse, portraying him as a "smooth talker" more intent on chasing women and working on his sideline construction business than on performing as a remote viewer. Schnabel hints that Morehouse's claim of the bullet episode giving him psychic powers was a fictional device Morehouse dreamed up as he began writing his book.

But there is much more to Schnabel's book.

It appears as though Stargate, for instance, owes the last several years of its existence to a love affair between a tarot card reader in the program and a chief aide of U.S. Senator Robert C. Byrd of West Virginia. Counsel Dick D'Amato, one of the most powerful non-elected officials in the U.S. government during Byrd's reigns as Senate Majority Leader, reportedly assured continuous Stargate funding even when some top military brass opposed it, according to Schnabel. If Schnabel's reporting is accurate, we have the extraordinary circumstance of a United States Senator from a conservative, religious state assuring public funding of a bizarre program employing psychics and practitioners of what many in that state would have considered in many cases to be "black arts."

Byrd is not the only senator listed as a supporter of the RV program. Revealing the non-partisan Senate Intelligence Committee support for the program, Schnabel lists current Secretary of Defense and then Republican Senator from Maine, William Cohen among the list of high-profile notables, along with former astronaut John Glenn (D-Ohio), Ted Stevens (R-Alaska), and Daniel Inouye (D-Hawaii).

UFOs and the "Dark Place"

There is also mention of UFOs in Schnabel's book.

Ed Dames and other RV'ers often encountered UFOs and their occupants, according to Schnabel. Dames seemed to prefer such sessions, writes Schnabel, and even garnered other RV'ers together to peek at ETs, the Loch Ness Monster, various Virgin Mary sites, and the lost continent of Atlantis, though Ingo Swann is reported to have eschewed most such endeavors to remote view UFOs because he feared the UFO occupants may turn the tables on him and not only remote view him, but possess his soul in the bargain.

If Schnabel's reportage is accurate on this last count, Swann's concerns carry implications for the existence of entities capable of "possessing" human beings, a belief persistent in nearly all civilizations and most major religions since the beginning of recorded history.

(Schnabel, after interviewing most of the major players in the RV program, reports that the RV program lost momentum in its later years and began a decline into "paranormal chaos, a dark place, infested by madness and mischievous sprites...")

It is not clear, but one is led to believe after reviewing these various books, that no one involved in the remote viewing programs paid much attention to such a possibility, whether the "possessing" entity was of a type we call extraterrestrial or an old-fashioned demon mentioned in various religious traditions. (For further details, see Chapter 3.) Assuming for the moment that such was a possibility, then we are presented a scenario whereby non-human intelligences invaded an initially promising human program and slowly turned it and many of its ill-equipped Jedi Knights toward the "Dark Side."

Monroe Training

One component of the remote viewing process developed by the government was a requirement for RV'ers to attend the Monroe Institute in Virginia. Through a process called "hemi-sync" developed by the Institute's founder, Robert Monroe, remote viewers were subjected to a regimen of sensory deprivation enhanced by sounds and music pumped through stereo headphones and designed to harmoniously attune the various spheres of the brain in order to facilitate altered states of consciousness, heightened awareness and even out-of-body experiences. Then, of course, there were the non-human intelligences to contend with.

In his now classic 1971 book *Journeys Out Of The Body,*[2] Monroe describes many encounters with such intelligences, including "helpers" that show up occasionally to aid a certain action. And then, there are other entities, like one described (Pages 142-144) as "attacking" him in "a no-holds-barred affair, silent, terrifyingly fast" as it "seemed to move from nerve center to nerve center, and some of the holds and pressures it applied were excruciating." Monroe reports fighting the entity "...for what seemed like hours" before he managed to "drop" back into his physical body and end the struggle.

The only way, he said, that he could return to sleep that night was to repeat this sentence at least 20 times: "My mind and body are open only to constructive forces; in the name of God and good, I am going into normal restful sleep." He later indicates that he was never able to discover "...any method, place, person, religious practice (that I would be sure of), drug, or anything else in my fund of knowledge, experience, and information that would absolutely guarantee protection against whatever attacked me."

A Similarity?

It is amazing to me the similarity in this experience expressed by Monroe and other contemporary stories related by dozens of people over time who reported being possessed by demons. Keeping the *Matrix of UFO Beliefs* (See Chapter One) in mind, we have to consider this a possibility. And in the context of remote viewing, who is to say—given the similarity of that process to the reported out-of-body experiences of others—that remote viewers weren't subjected to such onslaughts, knowingly or not? Supposing for a moment that demon possession is as real a possibility as aliens flying around in exotic spaceships (and perhaps even more so, given the incredible historic record of demons recorded over the centuries), then one begins to wonder of the "physics of the psychics" as the remote viewers left their corporeal bodies to visit distant targets and people. Does a person who practices leaving his/her body become more vulnerable to possession than one who does not? Does Monroe's "hemi-sync" process (if even unintentionally) somehow set up a person to be possessed? Could the "possession" referred to here really be a form of information virus present throughout history?

Monroe worried during his time as an out-of-body traveler that he could have had sex with discarnate spirits, not all that much different from ancient reports of succubi and incubi having sex with humans, and clearly similar to many modern "UFO abduction" reports.

Interesting, too, is Monroe's notion of there not being anything at his disposal that seemed to help him ward off such attacks as described above, even though later in the book he said the attacks became less frequent. He writes that the non-physical "helpers" he describes elsewhere in his book did not come to help him when he was being attacked by other entities which Monroe himself labeled "demons" (in quotes).

If the remote viewing program was infested with such entities or viruses, it's little wonder it spiraled into darkness and disarray, loosing its effectiveness and drawing plenty of wannabes like Marshall Applewhite and Bonnie Lu Nettles to it along the way.

A Final Personal Thought To This Chapter

It's inevitable when doing a book like this to wonder of one's own biases.

As for me, I do not attempt to incite fear or to impose my personal viewpoint (even if I state it) when I write about these various phenomena, although some of these subject areas can incite fear and do, indeed, induce strong viewpoints. What I do hope to accomplish with a book such as this is to encourage open minds and personal reflection. I and many of my friends over the course of the past several years have followed interesting paths, often finding ourselves and our paths intersecting, often not.

A very dear friend who practices Spirit Releasement Therapy (SRT) in Virginia recently began receiving training at the Monroe Institute. Another close friend who practices SRT and hypnotherapy and who holds a Ph.D. has already trained as a remote viewer, and I find his abilities quite impressive. He learned from one of the original government remote viewers, Lyn Buchanan, who offers an RV course through his business, PSI (Problems> Solutions> Innovations) in Mechanicsville, MD. Lyn once gave me and a few other friends a long lecture about remote viewing, then allowed us to try it. We all scored quite well. And I must admit I've often thought about taking Lyn's training. Ultimately, of course, one must wonder how one would use these techniques in everyday life. (Lyn says the process doesn't work in scrying lotto numbers—what a shame!)

I've now shared hypnotherapy with quite a few personal friends, some of whom were interested in examining recalled UFO incidents in their personal lives. In some instances, our lengthy sessions resulted in more clarity and understanding for the percipients, and sometimes not.

In one extreme case involving an acquaintance (I did not employ hypnosis or any other form of therapy, I was merely doing my bit as a reporter), we parted ways because she was convinced aliens were going to permanently take her away (at her choice) to a secret underground facility and employ her as a caretaker of hybrid children while she continued an intimate relationship with an alien. My bias at that point, which I argued quite forcefully, was for her to remain here among humans and to consider her experiences in light of the *Matrix of UFO Beliefs*, which I explained could help her consider a wide range of possibilities, from psychology to demonology to non-human intelligences to mind control (from whatever source) and many more, without needing to surrender her freedom and inalienable rights as a sentient being. Though the ETs, she said, had set a date for her departure then stiffed her, a fact which I pointed out as an example of "alien" (meaning "whatever its identity was") deception, she vociferously insisted that these aliens on their bad days were still far superior to humans on their good ones. We were both upset by each other's positions, and eventually she refused to discuss anything more with me. We haven't spoken since then. Very interesting how this phenomenon can often adversely affect human psychology and human relationships as a first course in manifesting itself. (Such does not require non-human involvement, either!)

And so, the wonder and pain, the mystery and evil, the tender and the tragic continue. Love must fight for a say-so, too. I only hope we can maintain human sovereignty and dignity in our rightful place in the grand scheme while we continue to examine the mystery and to confront our biases. Otherwise, it will come to another human-versus-human apocalypse of the type we've been forced to endure previously in our human history. In that vein, I react with an old, old bias: I pray for guidance for us all from the God of my fathers.

And one other bias: As I see it, the Heaven's Gate legacy is one of human death. Two more of the cult's followers attempted suicide, one successfully, in the weeks following the original event at Rancho Sante Fe, bringing the death toll so far to 40. There will probably be more. I prefer to explore for a world that offers hope for my little daughter and the future generations of humankind— a legacy of life.

I hope the mental health profession and all associated deprogrammers and healers can develop more and better ways to bolster such a legacy.

(1. *Remote Viewers: The Secret History of America's Psychic Spies,* Jim Schnabel, 1997, Dell Publishing, New York)
(2. *Journeys Out Of The Body,* Robert A. Monroe, 1971, Doubleday & Company, New York)

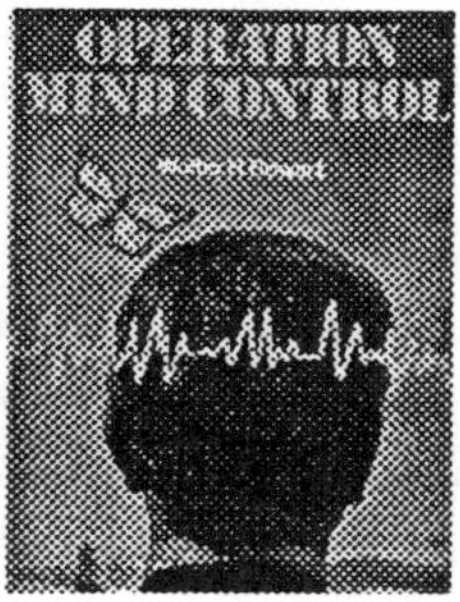

Chapter Seven

Who's Minding The Mind?

We have now arrived at a place that can induce squeamishness in some readers (if we haven't already!). It can also test one's credulity. But the bottom line is that there are real people researching and applying new technologies and methodologies involving mind influencing.

Mind control.

Said by many researchers to be the "crown jewels" of governments and their military/intelligence establishments, mind control links hand-in-hand with remote viewing (discussed in the previous chapter).

In its milder form, mind control (MC) is a voluntary act you submit yourself to every time you sit down in front of an active television set or a movie screen, or when you read a magazine or book, or when you surf the net, or practically any time you open your mind to any exterior medium. Images and symbols flood into your consciousness, the result of which is still hotly debated by psychologists, criminologists, sociologists, politicians, religious leaders and millions of parents, to name a few. Welcome to the doorstep of a new millennium—the age of information, entertainment and social control.

Another passive form of MC is hypnosis, which in and of itself is another form of (self) mind control, wherein a person harmonizes the conscious mind with the subconscious mind(s). "All hypnosis is self hypnosis" we are taught early during our hypnotherapy training. And as practiced by most hypnotherapists, that's exactly the way it works. Combine it with other things, though, and you step into the murky depths of mind abuse and MC.

In its more aggressive form, MC has, is and always will be as feared a weapon as any known to humankind. The very term carries terrifying implications—psychological abuse, a loss of control, induced paranoia and trauma—"walking death." Sometimes it doesn't appear to be so intimidating, like when it is lumped together with a new order of weapons referred to as "non-lethal."

As portrayed in mostly superficial documentaries and "edutainment" television programs (some of which are suspected of being propagandized by MC Central), non-lethal weapons appear to be the perfect tools for handling conflict during the politically correct years leading to a new millennium: Glues which can stick a military convoy fast to a roadway; rubber bullets or other projectiles shot from a gun that can stop an assailant (or a rioting prison inmate) without killing him or her; high frequency sound waves capable of frying electronic ignitions and equipment without frying their operators; even software viruses capable of destroying an enemy's entire information infrastructure without harming a single person. Quite an advance over only the space of a decade, when during the 1980s special weapons were developed to kill people while preserving inanimate structures.

In theory, at least, the non-lethal concept sounds good, in that it appears to be a kinder, gentler way to wage violence with a sort of no-harm, no-fault outcome.

However, the research being performed is not merely limited to glue, harmless bullets and software. There exists today technology to influence the human mind. When we're told this technology could be useful in quelling a prison riot or in subduing an aggressing enemy (even one sneaking into the back door of your house), what we're not told is that it also carries the potential of influencing each of us to become followers or believers, like say, on election day or during a military coup. Demonstrations of a Russian made "acoustic psychocorrection" system using electroencephalographs and a lowly 386 computer to influence subliminal perception have already taken place in the U.S. *Newsweek* magazine reported that the FBI secretly considered employing the equipment during the Waco standoff.[1]

The decades-long research and development of some of these "gee-whiz" technologies also overlooks the untold human suffering meted out and endured in the name of "progress" or "national security." You never know, but a victim of one or more of these experiments may be the next client to walk through your door.

While no firm figures are available, the U.S. government has already admitted to poisoning dozens of servicemen with radioactive fallout during nuclear weapons and related testing decades ago.[2] GIs were also unwittingly submitted to various other tests for medicinal research and a host of other experimental procedures, including biological weapons, over the past 50 years.

For a few such source references, you may wish to check the published findings of the May 6, 1994 U.S. Senate's Committee on Veterans' Affairs hearing, *"Is Military Research Hazardous to Veterans' Health? Lessons From World War II, The Persian Gulf, and Today,"* S. Hrg. 103-984; or the August 5, 1994 hearing, *"Reproductive Hazards and Military Service: What Are The Risks of Radiation, Agent Orange, and Gulf War Exposures?"*, S. Hrg. 103-983; or a December 8, 1994 staff report, *"Is Military Research Hazardous To Veterans' Health? Lessons Spanning Half a Century"* (S. Prt. 103-97), which admits: "During the last 50 years, hundreds of thousands of military personnel have been involved in human experimentation and other intentional exposures conducted by the Department of Defense (DOD), often without a servicemember's knowledge or consent."

Committee Chairman John D. Rockefeller, IV, (D-WV) writes in a forward to the last cited document: "During the last few years, the public has become aware of several examples where U.S. Government researchers intentionally exposed Americans to potentially dangerous substances without their knowledge or consent. The Senate Committee on Veterans' Affairs...has conducted a comprehensive analysis of the extent to which veterans participated in such research..."

Note the Senator points out that his committee looked only at victims who had served in the military, not in civilian populations. These reports also fail to pin the tail on the donkeys who perpetrated these abuses. Certainly, according to many reserachers, powerful incentives remain for those yet unidentified perpetrators to thwart further investigations and perhaps even to perpetuate hoaxes about UFOs as a way to cover "human abductions" or other mind games. It is not unusual, according to researcher W. H. Bowart (see below) for military personnel to experience "missing time," a hallmark for both Dissociative Identity Disorder patients and those alleging alien abduction.

In March, 1997, President Clinton instituted revised rules which were intended to stop any further secret experiments on unwitting humans, according to an announcement from the White House. And the government is reportedly settling court cases with families of the victims for estimated payments in the "hundreds of thousands of dollars," according to the New York Times.[3]

There are many more potential links of Mind Control to UFOs.

Most obvious, of course, is that many if not most abductees and contactees report feeling as if their minds are somehow controlled by the "aliens" involved in their experiences.

For a perspective on that, here is a report from a California hypnotherapist.

DISCUSSION

Are Abductees Being Brainwashed?

By Donna Higbee, CHt

Brainwashing... That is a strong word but I use it purposely, as I question the sudden change in abductees' attitudes all over the country. I'm a hypnotherapist in Santa Barbara and the director of CEIT (Contact Encounters Investigation Team), an abductee support and research group.

I noticed a drastic change earlier this year in the attitudes of several of the abductees from one meeting to the next. People who had been traumatized all their lives by ongoing abductions and had only anger and mistrust for their non-human abductors suddenly started saying they had been told/shown that everything that has happened to them was for their own good, that the abductors are highly spiritual beings and are helping them (the abductee) to evolve spiritually. By accepting this information, the abductees stopped fighting abduction and instead became passive and controlled.

When I checked with other researchers, I found that this was a pattern that was repeating itself over and over again around the country. I became concerned that abductees were accepting these explanations from entities that we know can be deceitful, use screen memories to mask real memories, use virtual reality scenarios to implant images into abductees' heads, and manipulate and abuse. I wrote an article for the *MUFON UFO Journal* (September 1995) and encouraged abductees to seriously think about what they were accepting as their truth, in light of the evidence, not the explanations offered them by these non-human entities. I invited comments from the readership.

The correspondence I received from other researchers reflected, for the most part, my own observations and feelings about this abductee attitude switch. But the letters I got from many abductees accused me of insulting their wonderful space brothers. I'd like to give a few quotes from some of the letters I received.

A non-abductee writes: "Growth is a personally achieved

occurrence from within one's own being, whether it is physical or spiritual. If these aliens are wanting us to believe that they are gifting humans with spiritual growth, I see this as a ploy for their own purposes. If this is not a tactic of their doings and is, instead, the abductees' way of justifying what has happened to them, then they are deluding themselves. Either way one looks at it, this is like justifying a cult leader who uses his members for experimentation and has sex with them for purposes he calls spiritual and sanctioned by God. We have seen this type of activity in human cults ... and have been appalled by it. What makes this same type of activity acceptable with aliens? Their actions speak for themselves."

One of the few abductees who agrees with me writes: "I was of this mindset a few years back and had to force myself to back away from it. I knew myself enough to know that it was not 'like me,' a very independent thinker, to be compliant or to trust so easily, but I do know programming when I see it. I still find myself being 'pulled' down the path of the 'Friendly and Caring' entity mindset, but the reality is - they are not. Their actions are not ethical. Like thieves in the night they have plundered our lives. If their intent was noble, they would not have to hide it. I agree, a spiritually advanced race would not behave as they do. It's pure logic and yet I still have to keep reminding myself of that. Up until 1992, I was incredibly compelled never to share my abduction experience with anyone; to do so would be a 'betrayal' of my 'space friends.' I cannot express how strongly compelled I was towards silence....to utterly, believing they were here for our benefit....Maybe it was because I went so much with the feeling of infatuation that I got to thinking, 'Whoa....listen to yourself...you sound like some kind of fanatic.' That's when it clicked. If anyone should've known better, it was me; and yet they still managed to manipulate me. I backed away from the entire issue and grew mistrustful of these idealistic proclivities both within myself and in literature I'd read. My only goal was to change my attitude towards them, and to see them for what they are. It took me two years to do this to the point where I could come into a group setting and even TALK about it! To do so would be betrayal! It was not and still is not easy, but I knew I had to stop protecting my 'captors' ....my 'abusers.'.....no matter what they said or promised me. It was hard for me to go from 'Special-Chosen-One' to 'Intergalactic

Mutineer' but the point is, I had to FORCE the resistance. I still do....and will, until our little cosmic terrorists fess up and become accountable for their actions."

Another abductee writes: "Once you've been cut open and can see your insides over and over, it becomes old hat. It's life!... Some people who experience abduction are always under their control. They need to be. How else can they be cared for? Or perhaps I should say monitored?"

A Native American wrote to me: "Native Americans are very aware of the beings that are 'visiting.' I have been told that they do not believe that these beings are extraterrestrial. In the old days the Star People visited and interacted with the people. Today the Wakan Sica (in Lakota), or the darker side, has come and has impersonated the Star People. This way they (the dark beings) could move into our culture, through the public fascination with UFOs."

An abductee writes: "Abduction is part of the grand plan ... the plan to change humans genetically so we will be able to adapt to a changing environment, such as that brought on by more radiation, more pollution, etc. At present our genes are breaking down under the stress but they are fixing all that. They will save us as a species and make us able to continue living here. We should be terribly thankful to them for all their help."

A MUFON State Director writes: ".... your article had an impact on me, for it put into words my own approach to abductions.... I suggest caution be the name of the game as we continue to explore the phenomenon. I, too, am unable to equate spirituality with taking someone against their will. Whatever the agenda may be surrounding alien abductions, I'm sure we are not being told the truth or, at the very least, being manipulated into cooperating with it."

An abductee writes: "How can you say we are being manipulated and controlled when we agreed to all this before we came into this life? In a pre-life arrangement, the one you call an abductee agreed to being used to aid his brothers from the other dimensions/planets. If this means experimentation, fetus removal and the like, then that is fine because it was all agreed to, the abductee has just forgotten the agreement. It will further his spiritual growth to be of service in such a manner."

Not an abductee himself but has an abductee in the family:

".... let's not be suckered into believing getting hit in the head with a baseball bat is fun. It could very well lead to our demise as an independent thinking race of beings. I feel one of the greatest gifts we have is our independence as individuals. I won't give up my independence without a fight."

An abductee writes: "If abductees are more at peace by accepting their abductors as spiritual, what's wrong with that? Abductee brainwashing? I don't think so. The body is controlled, not ones feelings."

A researcher: "Your paper dovetails nicely with a lot of information that I have gathered. I really appreciate your using the terms 'brainwashing' and 'kidnapping' because that is exactly what is going on. Furthermore, the word brainwashing aptly describes the veracity of this experience. One of your major theses is that abductees themselves are changing their stories from feeling traumatized and abused to finding new-found enlightenment and deep spirituality. What is indeed amazing is not only the drastic change of the abductees' new-found tolerance but that they themselves don't realize that they have been deceived."

An abductee writes: "My first memory was so wonderful. At first I was scared but then a woman (alien) lifted me out of my crib and held me ... and said 'You're my baby now.' ....They control my body and what it does but they don't control my mind. I make my own opinions. .... If there is a problem, they fix it. They watch over me. They are my God."

Feelings and opinions on abduction run the gamut and we certainly have no set answers. However, I continue to question the motives of the abductors and their behavior. I would strongly suggest that every abductee do the same. The question was asked above— why not believe that the abductors are spiritual if it makes you feel better?

My answer to her is "because it's not the truth."

(I welcome comments and thoughts regarding the above article. I can be reached at the following address: Donna Higbee, Post Office Box 6404, Santa Barbara, California 93160. Email address: Goodhigbee@aol.com)

More Discussion

One-On-One Interview With Budd Hopkins

By Dick Farley (Copyright ©1996)

(GREENSBORO, NC — July 7) When Budd Hopkins and I sat down to lunch at the Cafe Expresso in the hotel hosting the Mutual UFO Network's 1996 convention, it wasn't the first time we'd met.

Budd and I have been in loose touch since 1987, after publication of his second book about perceived "alien abduction" experiences, *Intruders*. (His first book on the topic, *Missing Time*, had appeared in 1981.)

And before that, in one of those "coincidences" which veteran "UFO" researchers, scholars and journalists eventually come to accept as part of the territory, Budd and I are from the same home town.

Not only the same home town, (Wheeling, WV), but actually from the same neighborhood (Meadow Estates), where Budd and his older brother Stewart grew up, and where I later grew up.

While older brother Stewart remained in Wheeling to take over the family's Chrysler-Plymouth dealership (Hopkins Motors), Budd, after graduating from Oberlin College in Ohio, "beat feet" to the Big Apple in pursuit of full expression of his inner muses on the New York art scene.

Eventually scoring some successes by having his pieces hang in the Guggenheim (modern art museum) and, perhaps more helpfully, in the pads of well-heeled art patrons, Budd says that after he had a 1964 "UFO" sighting, his interest in the subject was piqued.

As perhaps West Virginia's currently preeminent "UFO guy," and with a long-awaited book about a purported Manhattan abduction with multiple witnesses (the "Linda Cortile" case), Budd and I sat down over lunch in Greensboro to chat.

With his marriage to a very nice lady approaching, and with his new book *(Witnessed)* slated for publication in August, Budd was his usual kind and candid self. And, as is also a hallmark of this West Virginian, Budd Hopkins had some surprising things to say...

DF: Where do you see the UFO field heading, and more specifically what do you hope *Witnessed* will contribute?

BH: What I'm hoping is that when people are confronted with a case like this, they'll realize there are only two options.

Either it's a hoax, with many people going to an awfully lot of trouble and expense to set it up, or it actually happened. After six years of research we have more than 20 people who either were involved in it or were witnesses to it.

And if it did actually happen, then it is important. And it has to be considered fairly, as well as what is being reported by thousands and thousands of people all around the world as happening to them.

DF: Your views about "alien abductions," as to what seems to be taking place and why, are quite well known. How do you expect *Witnessed* to influence the general UFO field?

BH: As I said, these scenarios are being reported by people all over the world. And the recent publicity about that new movie, ("Independence Day," which Budd had not yet seen) shows that there is great public interest... maybe even an 'obsession'... in this phenomenon.

I hope *Witnessed* will help do two things, primarily.

First, I'm hoping a case like this will, in effect, "give people permission" to demand that these events be taken seriously, and enormously support the idea that we need to look into it intelligently.

Secondly, I'd like to pry loose more people from government who have information that pertains to these occurrences, to present enough logical and clear-cut evidence so people interested are free to pursue it all wherever it may lead.

DF: Do you believe the government knows more than it's told?

BH: Maybe so. But I think the government is panicked and has been. They don't know what to do.

As far as the government being in cahoots with aliens, I think that's b**ls**t. The aliens don't need anybody's permission to do what they're doing.

But I am greatly disturbed at the government's participation in the cover-up, and the damage that it's done to millions of lives.

DF: How so?

BH: What if the government took this same approach to, say, another issue entirely, like a separate more worldly crime, like rape?

Imagine the damage that would be done if, despite the evidence and the obvious trauma exhibited by victims, government authorities refused to acknowledge that the crime even existed, let alone had been committed against the person making the complaint.

That's how the abduction phenomenon has been treated, and the damage that's been done to so many people seeking only help and a degree of understanding is unconscionable.

DF: This brings us to your views about the nature of what is going on, and what might be its purpose. More importantly, how should we as a people feel about it, assuming that it is real? John Mack's position, as he restated here (at MUFON '96) last night, is that these ostensible alien entities have come to Earth "to save us," or at least to save the planet from our excesses. Do you agree with John?

BH: I've known John for several years, since being introduced to him by Robert Jay Lifton, after which I helped to spark his interest in this field. And John and I remain very good friends, in fact we had breakfast together this morning. But I disagree with him strongly on this aspect of what might be going on, at a couple of levels.

First, maybe because John is a psychiatrist and has spent his working life dealing with people who are, by definition, in some kind of distress needing psychological help, he sees our species as being in a state of spiritual atrophy.

But perhaps because I come at life from the perspective of an artist, looking at the edges and fringes of human experience as being part of our enrichment, I just don't see or feel that atrophy.

DF: So, if the aliens are not coming here, as John Mack believes, to uplift and transform us and our planet for "our own good," why do you personally think it's all happening?

BH: I've always felt they (the aliens) are coming here because they need *our* spirit.

I don't really see this as if we (humanity) are gaining spiritually from their activities and interactions with us.

DF: Whoa! What are you saying here? These guys are parasites?

BH: I just mean I've never seen anything coming in from the aliens to make me think we're getting anything from it at all.

Sure, to many experiencers the memories have had an impact, which some translate into deeper meanings for their lives. In a way, that's like many Vietnam veterans who have had overall a deeper, richer experience in life than, say, a hardware store clerk in Ohio who had never left home. But that doesn't mean Vietnam was overall a benevolent enrichment of the veteran's experience.

DF: So this is where you differ from John Mack in your "take" on why the aliens are here?

BH: That's right. I've never seen any sign that the aliens bring any attitude of real benevolence. And I think John's error is to assume that this spiritual growth some abductees are feeling is from "them," (the aliens). It may be from us.

DF: Can you expand on that?

BH: Let's look at our astronauts as a kind of 'control group.' Here are folks who are "taken away" as a group, and from space they almost uniformly have reported "transformations" in their world views, as well as of their personal approaches to life. And they've all come back feeling very protective of our planet.

It's the same kind of question one has to ask about seemingly "channelled" material, whether it comes from a source other than ourselves... or maybe from an aspect of ourselves which we don't usually acknowledge or allow to "speak" to us.

We shrink the human spirit to think that all of it has to come from "out there."

All of that idea, that help comes from outside, is not unlike a fundamentalist approach to traditional religious experience.

The basic "UFO message" has been pretty much the same since the earliest "contactee" reports back in the 1950s. And this may be our human reaction to our perception of their being here, not that they may not be taking some advantages of that.

DF: But you don't believe that is their intent, to help us?

BH: No. I just don't see this as if we're gaining spiritually from them or their being here.

DF: Well, then, it seems as if your view is more consistent with the theme of the new movie, "Independence Day," where the aliens are here to take over the human race, but we finally get our act together enough to blow them out of our skies. John Mack told the MUFON convention crowd last night that he was disappointed by the movie and its "American can-do" message of technological triumph over the aliens. So do you believe Earth is being invaded, given what you have written previously about their human-alien hybridization program?

BH: No, I don't believe at this point that we're dealing with an 'invasion.' The whole situation, from what I gather, is more misleading than that, not so clear cut, but I can't speculate more than anyone else as to its ultimate purpose or eventual outcome.

DF: Well, if you aren't ready to welcome these aliens with open arms, as John Mack and those of his perspective suggest, what do you believe we humans ought to do?

BH: I would like to see Earth have a sort of resistance to these kinds of events and whatever or whoever is carrying them out. Not in a warlike way, but in a way that demands respect for our own status as living beings with a right to live as we see fit on our own planet, for better or for worse.

Darker Human Involvements

Darker human involvements in the UFO phenomenon are reported by a number of sources, wherein it is suggested that "UFO abductions" are actually the result of a continuing, highly sophisticated military/intelligence mind control research operation which has stretched over decades in the U.S. and Canada, and which is able to "brainwash" then program victims in order for them to perform acts of espionage, sexual prowess, and perhaps even murder without their direct conscious awareness, or without recall. If later the victims begin to experience psychological problems for which they seek help, they may begin to exhibit dissociated conditions revolving around an alien abduction scenario instead of the actual human brainwashing/programming experience. Some healers using hypnosis and others using "deprogramming" protocols have claimed to have broken through clients' induced amnesia to find the mind-washing events, as well as the identities of the human perpetrators.

Entering into the mix is a debate over the validity of recalled memories. Advocates say memories retrieved under hypnosis and/or regression oriented therapies are sufficient to help a client heal. Meanwhile, the False Memory Syndrome Foundation (FMSF) has begun to systematically argue that such retrieved memories are false, or in the least are unreliable. (See Sidebar: False Memory Syndrome)

Further complicating the matter are a number of sources which contend that the FMSF is administered in part by some of the very people who originated or participated as researchers in mind control research.

The Books: A Review

With such suspicion and distrust as exists today, there is no surprise to learn of an extant and growing underground—particularly evident nowadays on the Internet—of MC researchers and groups. Literature on the subject is exploding, although one is challenged when trying to authenticate it.

There are some publications, however, which appear to piece together credible, if troubling MC etiologies. A sampling of the available literature can be found in two books, *Operation Mind Control,* a 1977 tome recently updated to over 700 pages as a Limited Researcher's Edition by its author, Walter H. Bowart, and

Psychic Dictatorship In The U.S.A., by Alex Constantine. A third source which appears to lend credibility to this discussion is the published version of a lecture, "The Greenbaum Lecture on Ritual Abuse, MPD and Mind Control" by D. C. Hammond, Ph.D., a psychologist at the University of Utah. (It also appears as if various victim groups are now forming with the intent of heightening public awareness and of bringing political pressure to rectify past sins.) I'll briefly review these three sources, but I encourage you to locate copies of your own to adequately plumb their reach. One thing the two books have in common is adequate bibliographic underpinnings that can lead you to more background. Such research will in all probability directly influence the way you will approach therapy with UFO percipients from now on.

Operation Mind Control: The Cryptocracy's Plan to Psycho-civilize You (Limited Researcher's Edition) By W. H. Bowart, 1978 (Dell first edition), 1994 revised second edition, Flatlands Editions, P. O. Box 2420, Fort Bragg, CA 95437. Available for free along with 12 issues of the FOTF newsletter with a charter membership ($100) in the Freedom Of Thought Foundation. E-Mail: freetht@azstarnet.com

Bowart, a journalist/novelist currently working on a documentary version of *OMC*, is also an Advisory Board member of the Freedom of Thought Foundation (FOTF, POB 35072, Tucson, Az, 85740-5072). The book declares the FOTF to be "an ad hoc committee of survivors, researchers, therapists, deprogrammers, counselors, lawyers, doctors and civil right activists" that wishes to "evolve into a reliable referral service so that more survivors can be directed to qualified deprogrammers and that more therapists, doctors and counselors can learn the efficient technologies to help victims of classical trauma-based programming. In the long term we hope that it will also become an effective political organization to curb human experimentation and attacks on the human mind on both an individual and collective basis."

The book begins with a note to the second edition:

A Warning to Survivors!

"This book contains information that will trigger you. Give it to your deprogrammer, rather than try to read it yourself unless you have a thoroughly reintegrated personality."

The book then moves into a Foreword by a preeminent and pioneer MC researcher, Richard Condon, author of *The Manchurian Candidate*. Condon attests to Bowart's efforts to obtain documentation for the book, including many Freedom of Information requests, in an effort to reveal what he sees as the book's central theme: "W. H. Bowart has proven each step of this official, terminal, government anarchy... To alter and control human minds is the ultimate anarchy. What is offered by official apologists as a tribute to the deeds of daring-do by romantic spies are acts of hatred and sadism against all people in an insane and degraded determination to extirpate conscience from society."

Chapter One begins with Bowart's systematic portrayal of various mind control victims, mostly military men in the beginning, and in later chapters, civilians. He outlines the methods used on the victims, as the victims were able to recall them. He brings in corroborating sources, then highlights various identifiable government programs and projects involved in mind control. At one point (Chapter 10) he then reprints what he says is Army Major Michael A. Aquino and Col. Paul E. Vallely's paper entitled, "From PSYOP to MindWar: The Psychology of Victory," in which the pair propose a new thrust in the military's interest in so-called "psychotronic research." The paper offers this chilling paragraph:

> "Psychotronic research is in its infancy, but the U.S. Army already possesses an operational weapons system designed to do what LTC Alexander [note: John Alexander, a retired Army non-lethal weapons expert who is now reportedly connected with a UFO research consortium in Nevada] would like ESP to do—except that this weapons system uses existing communications media. It seeks to map the minds of neutral and enemy individuals and then to change them in accordance with U. S. national interests. It does this on a wide scale, embracing military units, regions, nations, and blocs. In its present form it is called Psychological Operations (PSYOP)."

After making an argument as to why the authors don't think

the term "Psyop" to project enough fear for potential enemies, they suggest the term "MindWar" be substituted. They then point out tried and true propaganda methods, interweaving them with more exotic means of turning heads:

> "There are some purely natural conditions under which minds may become more or less receptive to ideas, and MindWar should take full advantage of such phenomena as atmospheric electromagnetic activity, air ionization and extremely low frequency waves."

After a keen analysis of the paper showing linkages to, among other things, Nazism, Bowart offers this additional information about one of the authors, provided here to illustrate how such belief systems seem able to inculcate themselves through the strata of a country:

> "...Michael A. Aquino was a disciple of Anton Levey's Church of Satan for ten years. The C of S was among a half dozen Satanist churches and organizations which were influenced by the magical secrets of National Socialism in Germany. A number of radical-right groups had tried to ally themselves with The Church of Satan, including the American Nazi party and Robert Shelton's United Klans of America. Publicly, LaVey had maintained his distance. Secretly, there was reason to believe that a strong bond existed."

Aquino's involvement extends well beyond MindWar and even affiliation with the Church of Satan, according to Bowart.

Why do such excerpts belong in a small book about UFOs and mental health? To wit:

> "The disclosures of Paul Bonacci [an MC victim], which jibe with reports of MPD professionals in other cases, point to several peculiar artificially induced memories common to many Monarch [a MC project

> concerned with 'perverted sexuality, bestiality, ritual abuse, trauma...' identified in Bowart's book) victimized children. Chaitkin [Anton Chaitkin, a reporter for *The New Federalist*] said that a number of the victims were recovering 'memories of tormentors dressed as space aliens...'"

Bowart provides a dizzying number of stories to illustrate the existence of active mind control programs and programming scenarios extant in this country. Perhaps most valuable is an extensive Appendices, a thorough Index, and a detailed bibliography. Chapter 40 highlights conversations during an amazing "secret conference" of an "emergency panel of five psychiatrists and clinical psychologists" who "met to discuss the alarming data they were gathering about mind control, satanic ritual abuse, and alien programming from patients diagnosed as suffering from MPD." This chapter alone is worth whatever it takes for therapists to get the book, as it presents a credible discussion by mental health professionals of procedures for differential diagnoses and treatment options.

When I contacted Mr. Bowart about my book, he sent the following e-mail reply (excerpted):

"Be sure you don't overlook the stats on the number of dissociative cases in among the 'abductees.' Tests that have been given indicate it to a high percentage. See ALIEN DISCUSSIONS, the MIT thing. You might want to include Dr. G.L. Dean's comparison from the back of OPERATION MIND CONTROL, Appendix E."

I agree with his advice to check out the relevant parts of the proceedings, *Alien Discussions,* of the 1992 M.I.T. conference, though I don't have space here to do so.

Here is a brief summary of Applendix E in Mr. Bowart's book:

Part One consists of 11 Tables contrasting "Alien Abduction Accounts" with "RA [Ritual Abuse] Accounts." It is not reported how many cases were used as the basis for compiling the tables, a factor which, of course, could heavily influence the results. However, taken at face value, these tables can be quite valuable to a therapist because such data can possibly help one more accurately diagnose presenting problems.

The tables compare major categories of the accounts, and

include "Patterns," "Elements" (paraphernalia), "Messages Given," "Psychological Sequelae," "Locations for Experience," "Personal History," "Timetable," "Wounds and Scars Observed," "Violations Against Free Will," and "Philosophy & Beliefs."

Part Two consists of three chronological charts which are presented side by side over several pages, and which highlight events in the following categories:

1. History of Psychiatry & World Events including Mafia Development in the United States;
2. History of MPD, Trauma, Dissociation; New Clinical Syndromes; Groups Opposing Recovered Memories;
3. Mind Control Research; Medical Abuses & Emergence of Alleged UFO Sightings, Alien Abduction & Ritual Abuse Phenomena

While the information clearly suggests complimentary development and/or perhaps "cause and effect" scenarios for various of the three categories, it lacks adequate explanatory text to help put the various events in context. There is almost the appearance of randomness to these charts that not only distracts, but which confuses as well unless the reader is fully aware of the historical development of these various events in the first place. Nonetheless, this section, too is a valuable reference for a therapist because it is evident that certain of the entries suggest contributing factors which may continue to influence your clients and the development of your methodologies. Parts of the whole are fascinating if subjective, as one is presented a model which seemingly suggests a complimentary and simultaneous growth and sophistication of Mind Control technology and UFOs.

The chart containing the growth of psychiatry is interesting, namely because as we saw earlier with the book *Ecopsychology* (Chapter 4) proposing to allow a small handful of people to redefine "sanity," and with Dr. John Mack calling for the "invention of a new psychology" according to narrow beliefs and parameters, we see others throughout history who have to one degree or another accomplished precisely that goal.

Operation Mind Control (the Limited Researcher's Edition) offers over 700 pages of information. It reflects the efforts of a brave man dedicated to uncovering perhaps the most heinous (and one of the most pervasive) social phenomenon in the world today.

This is not to say that *OMC* couldn't use some editing of extant text and the introduction of some additional information. There does appear to be a few deficiencies, evidenced by a lack of sections devoted to the development of eugenics, for instance, or a section highlighting both the psychology associated with the UFO phenomenon, and a broader discussion of UFOs as they pertain to MC. In correspondence with Mr. Bowart, it would appear as if he does possess much of this. Though mentioned selectively, I would like to see a more comprehensive portrayal of the money sources behind the development of MC and associated venues. The bibliography may help assuage some this concern, but textual summaries would strengthen the overall presentation, in my opinion. In all, *OMC* is a keeper, a break-through effort that offers the most thorough and well documented overview of Mind Control on the planet.

Psychic Dictatorship in the U.S.A., 1995, Feral House, ISBN 0922915288, $12.95 by Alex Constantine

From the blurb on the back cover:

> "Bombing minds rather than bodies is the warfare of the new millennium. Alex Constantine's explosive book uncovers the terrifying extent of electromagnetic and biotelemetric mind control experimentation on involuntary human subjects in America today. Funded under the euphemism of 'Non-Lethal Technology,' the Pentagon has developed the ability to transmit voices, and inflict pain, madness, even death, with the push of a button.
>
> "*Psychic Dictatorship* tracks the use of cults by intelligence organization [*sic.*] as cover for arms sales, mind control and even child abuse to create assassins with multiple personality syndrome... [the book's] wide-ranging contents veer from the esoteric to the everyday."

Thus you have the essence of author/radio commentator Alex Constantine's book.

What the back cover doesn't tell you, however, is that to begin any assessment of Alex Constantine's work, you should first begin with a knowledge of the False Memory Syndrome Foundation, for Constantine is to the FMSF as a gunslinger is to a tin can sitting atop a fence post.

For example, early on in the book (Page 25) he relates the

following:

"The fact is that the wave of ritual child abuse allegations that swept the country in the 1980s cloaked federal psychotronic and eugenics experiments on young children. As one adult survivor of psychotronic mind control concludes, 'covert arms of government...have coined the term "screen memories" to describe the obfuscational memories impressed by the abusers themselves.' The so-called 'False Memory Syndrome,' he says, 'is a scapegoat created by a consortium of federal "spin doctors" bent on negating the believability and viability of the more than 12,000 unwitting citizens who have been on the receiving end of this technology.'

"The 'false memory' bromide has been popularized largely by organized pedophiles, cultists and hired guns of psychiatry. It has been adopted as the status quo position of the press. But the cover story originated with the CIA's mind control netherworld. 'Nazi-inspired scientists,' the survivor says, 'perform medical tests during the abuse event, such as implantation of biotelemetric tracking devices into nasal cavities and ear canals.'"

Thus, a portion of *Psychic Dictatorship* is devoted to dismantling the FMSF.

Constantine, among others, argues that most so-called "alien abductions" are in fact kidnappings perpetrated by various government agencies and/or organized groups or cults which implant memories of alien abductions in victims' minds as a way to cover their schemes. Successful remote viewing, he asserts, is the result of telemetric brain technology developed by the same agencies. In supporting his thesis throughout the

***Sidebar:* Implants Off The Shelf**

As an aside, in the second edition of another book, *Underground Bases and Tunnels: What is the government trying to hide?*, Richard Sauder, Ph.D., provides background and schematics of UFO-like technology that is shown to be quite terrestrial, at least in its application. One such item is an inexpensive tracking device available to farmers to inject into cattle or pets. Sauder points out that this "...is now a technology in commercial use that almost precisely mirrors the needle-injected implants said to be inserted into abductees by aliens." In that regard, he says, "I think we have to at least consider the possibility that some of these reported aspects of abductions may actually be earthly technologies used by terrestrial humans to radically alter a subject's perception of reality during an 'alien abduction' experience."

Sidebar: THE FALSE MEMORY SYNDROME

As a therapist, you should already be quite familiar with the false memory syndrome as an extension of a long held acknowledgment of what psychologists have recognized as "confabulation." I will not go into great detail here, but merely highlight the syndrome and the now powerful foundation built around it.

The so-called false memory syndrome rests on the assumption that memories fade over time and are subject to alteration by various means including suggestion. This tendency then makes memory vulnerable to implantation of so-called "false" memories. In a number of spectacular court cases, former clients of therapists have successfully won huge settlements by claiming the therapists introduced into their minds "false memories" such as childhood abuse, ritual abuse, incest and the like which were at variance with actual historic facts. (Case law, however, is still quite unclear on the subject.)

Further, and in a new wrinkle according to an article by well known FMS advocate and author Elizabeth F. Loftus in the September, 1997 *Scientific American*,[1] "...false incriminating evidence can induce people to accept guilt for a crime they did not commit and even to develop memories to support their guilty feelings."

In reaction to the emerging concept of false memory, the False Memory Syndrome Foundation was founded in the 1980s, and is now attempting to both educate and persuade society of what the FMSF claims to be growing proof of the syndrome.

The quite numerous but apparently not as well organized nor funded opponents of the FMSF, perhaps even representing the vast majority of therapists, argue the invalidity of the syndrome when memories are connected to trauma. They also point out that the FMS debate has had a deleterious effect in keeping victims of true abuse from either reporting the crimes or from seeking therapeutic relief, thus allowing abusive perpetrators to remain at large while the victims continue suffering. And finally, some opponents like Alex Constantine contend the Foundation is peopled at least in part by many mental health workers and/or mind control experts and intelligence officers with a dark history of perpetrating psychiatric abuse against unwitting human subjects.

Given that the vicious FMS debate is continuing, it is hard to predict an outcome, though one subtle implication may in fact become even more dominant in the profession: pharmacological companies will increasingly be offering more and more "psych cures in a bottle" as more and more therapists retreat from the field, as more and more insurance companies raise both malpractice rates and reimbursement parameters, and as more and more lawyers discover the potentially lucrative rewards of successfully pressing FMS cases.

Given the at best "soft" scientific nature of psychology, what with some 500 variant modalities available for a practitioner to employ, it would appear as though the FMS debate may well cripple or perhaps even destroy book, complete with revealing a brief history of MC in this century, Constantine offers many direct statements by researchers, including a 1973 *Psychology Today* article which quotes an M.I.T. professor as bemoaning a "narrow, unrealistic view of human social behavior" on the part of neuro- and behavioral scientists, a fact which could lead the development of 'psychotechnology' to the point of becoming 'a favorite tool of social and political repression.'"

More recently, Constantine says, money to fund the development of electromagnetic (EM) weapons capable of inducing some forms of MC was expended through research for the 1980s SDI (Star Wars) missile defense system. He says one physicist, Paul Brodeur, "...examined a schematic for an 'Electron Beam Accelorator' of the type to be incorporated—supposedly—in space-based defense. Brodeur discovered that the weapon was in reality a device capable of generating a powerful EM pulse."

Constantine, like Bowart (see above) provides historical background to the development of modern day mind control which can be traced, at least in part these and other authors contend, to Hitler Germany, where brutal psychological and physiological experimentation on large groups of humans, mostly Jews, were routinely carried out.

An oblique but relevant cross reference to such assertions comes from a rather surprising source, *Popular Mechanics*, which ran a story in August, 1997 about a covert operation termed "Project Paperclip." Also surprising was the context of the piece, in which the magazine speculates a connection between Nazi scientists and the real explanation for the so-called "Roswell UFO Crash" of 1947, which the magazine says had nothing to do with an alien craft, but rather with a quite terrestrial one, a "lifting platform" developed by the Nazi scientists in league with Japanese experts brought to this country.

Sidebar: **The False Memory Syndrome (cont.)**

significant portions of the profession in the long run, a blessing or a catastrophe, depending on one's perspective. However, if there are in fact perpetrators and their associated financiers hiding behind this debate in order to cover their own dark history, then people like Alex Constantine, W. H. Bowart, Cory Hammond and a host of others will eventually find them out.

Constantine's book does have its flaws.

First, there is no index, a problem more of the publisher's than of the author's, but a terrible oversight nonetheless, in that it places a true hardship on a reader interested in tracking names and events mentioned throughout the book. And it makes the book appear less credible, too. In as fringe an area as this, where mere appearances can determine the fate of a book, the absence of an index can send a reference book into the wastebasket. The front cover nearly has a "comic book look" to it (again the problem of the publisher), thus further eroding interest and credibility. Regretfully, modern mainstream publishers seem averse to publishing books like these.

And second, like Bowart, Constantine is willing to regard UFO abduction scenarios only as covers for covert mind control exercises without also considering such scenarios in broader contexts as presented in Chapter One of this book.

All in all, though, *Psychic Dictatorship* is a valuable reference, as it goes hand-in-hand with the Bowart work reviewed above. Together, and despite their apparent flaws, these two books can lead you via sourced documentation and wide bibliography into as much depth as you wish on the subject of mind control.

The Greenbaum Lecture On Ritual Abuse, MPD and Mind Control

Originally entitled "Hypnosis in MPD: Ritual Abuse," this lecture reportedly was delivered at the June 25, 1992 Fourth Annual Eastern Regional Conference on Abuse and Multiple Personality, in Alexandria, Virginia, and was sponsored by the Center for Abuse, Recovery & Empowerment.

It is interesting that if, like me, you call the Center and inquire about obtaining a copy of this lecture, you will likely be told that it is not available due to legal considerations. It's also interesting that if like me, you repeatedly call the presenter, Dr. D. Corydon Hammond, Ph.D. a psychologist and Research Associate Professor of Physical Medicine and Rehabilitation (in addition to a long string of other job responsibilities and positions) on staff at the University of Utah Medical Center and leave a message of your intentions to obtain a copy of the lecture and to ask a few questions about it, you will likely never hear from him. There are many copies of the lecture around, and my guess is you could probably find it on the net. It's worth the search.

I felt it important to include a mention of the lecture here because it provides valuable insight into certain methods of detecting programming alleged to be used on ritually abused victims. It also provides some excellent cross references and sources. And it even mentions UFOs, again as conveniently implanted memories to cover over actual ritual MC experiences.

The Lecture

Dr. Hammond reports stumbling across some heavy cult programming in clients of his while he was employing hypnosis. He then began to find ways of unraveling the programming, while simultaneously finding himself at the center of a growing network of others who were discovering the same thing. The result, according to Dr. Hammond, is that "I have gone from someone kind of neutral and not knowing what to think about it all to someone who clearly believes ritual abuse is real, and that the people who say it isn't are either naïve like people who didn't want to believe the Holocaust or—they're dirty."

Dr. Hammond then intimates in his lecture that he became the target of death threats, but that he "finally decided to hell with them. If they're going to kill me, they're going to kill me. It's time to share more information with therapists."

He then offers an opinion that from one-half to two-thirds of all ritual abuse patients have been exposed to some common form of programming, a startling figure for sure. He says it seemed to originate with one principal source, a young Hasidic Jewish boy who was well schooled in Cabalistic mysticism and who worked with Nazi death camp doctors who were also Satanists. These doctors and the boy, he says, were brought to America by U.S. intelligence experts, where they were allowed to continue their mind-control research in military hospitals. From there, the boy grew up and began practicing a now fully mature programming and mind control regime on hundreds of unwitting subjects, especially children. The cult prospered and spread, Dr. Hammond observes.

The central programming, he believes, revolves around a core regimen of encoded words, symbols and phrases. Once a client is in altered state, Dr. Hammond can repeat a few key words, the client's reaction to which will indicate the presence of "formal, intensive brainwashing and programming," he says.

From there, a formal deprogramming regimen can begin, an overview of which he provides in his lecture.

(1. *Newsweek*, "A Subliminal Dr. Strangeglove," date unknown. The Human Potential Foundation, Inc. sponsored Dr. Smirnov and an assistant to visit this country to demonstrate their system in March,1993.)
(2. *NY Times*, National Report page 7, col. 6, "Rule Adopted to Prohibit Secret Tests on Humans," March 29, 1997)
(3. *ibid*)

Chapter Eight

Doing Something About It

So far, we've taken a quick trip across the landscape of extant UFO-related belief systems. The *Matrix of UFO Beliefs* has been fleshed out sufficiently enough to allow us to explore ways of helping our clients in ways we perhaps had not considered previously.

My bottom line viewpoint, having intensely researched UFOs now for a number of years and having become acquainted with some of the phenomenon's more toxic, if alluring, aspects is that one is best served in this research when maintaining a high tolerance for ambiguity, a low threshold for bull-crap, and a next to zero allowance for "revealed truth." Without a viable framework on which to assemble a broad tapestry of possible UFO beliefs for examination, one is left to wander among a labyrinthine maze of possibilities, many of which can seduce your clients into a belief system that can, by slow and barely perceptible increments, erode their faith (religious, philosophical, political and otherwise) and replace it with an alluring if false spiral leading in its most diabolical way toward any number of psychological problems, even premature and self-inflicted death. That's why the *Matrix* is so important. Had the Heaven's Gate adherents been in possession of the *Matrix* and understood it, or at least had they broadly considered all aspects of this enigmatic phenomenon while resisting a desire to *believe* in any limited part of it, they may well have found options other than the tragic one they chose on March 26, 1997.

The point to all of this is not to condemn people like Whit Strieber, John Mack or any of the others mentioned in a negative light in this book. Witch hunts, mercifully, are a thing of the past. Besides, **it appears as if we are all vulnerable to the sorts of energies with which these people deal publicly.**

If *any* of these energies is real, then perhaps *all of them* are real, negative, positive and in between, at least in the way they play out in our 3-D existence.

It sure seems as if these are powerful energies we're dealing with, powerful enough to sway us in directions we can't always anticipate or even realize. Even the best scientists, and perhaps the people previously mentioned here are scientists in some regard, even the best scientists are not immune from sometimes catching the diseases or viruses they study.

Some even spread the viruses without knowing it. They base their actions on certain beliefs, one of which is to believe they cannot be negatively affected by this phenomenon they study and appreciate. As subtle as these viruses, biological or informational, are, though, such surety of belief may well be the first symptom of an "infection."

Along with the more benevolent aspects of the phenomenon, there is also a more aggressive, sometimes hostile always beguiling aspect that appears for all its worth to be representing a war, a quiet war, one that seeks to win and control *your* perceptions. Few guns are needed in this war, because the field of battle takes place within your mind. The only volleys exchanged here are quite subdued, a few salvos of purported information gently inculcated into your consciousness by the repetitive, monotonous and persistent urging of a point of view—a whisper lobbed onto the fertile and rich loam of your imagination. This is a war with the subtlety of an eyelash striking a cymbal, a victory declared with the successful communication of an image, a thought, or a fleeting glimpse of what Dr. J. Allen Hynek called "high strangeness."

We, all of us, believer, debunker, skeptic, agnostic are somehow involved in the conflict. There are no neutral parties here.

Issues are arising from the analysis of UFO experiences that must not be left exclusively to the tabloids nor to the 'true believers.' Nor can these issues be left to obscure scientists, to certain professions or to government agencies with, shall we say, less than spotless records of their historical dealings with the province of the human mind. This war, like all others, concerns an effort to win the hearts and minds of people— in this case an entire planetary population, **including YOU**— but we cannot abdicate responsibility for interpretation and meaning of it and leave it to the manipulation of modern day prophets, priest kings or other interpreters of truth. This information is too valuable, and yet sometimes to toxic for that. So, while we must discover a place of truth for ourselves, this phenomenon must, in the true spirit of Jeffersonian Democracy, be openly and aggressively analyzed, discussed and debated by the American people and the world population as a whole.

To do otherwise, to blithely insist that people like the 39 who died in California were "crazy" without also considering the "culture of death" which perhaps drove them to their radical belief system, is to help prepare the way for the next Heaven's Gate tragedy.

As a healer, you have it in your power to do something positive about it.

If you haven't treated a client expressing connections between a perceived "UFO" experience and his or her presenting problems, my guess is that you will. And if you have treated such clients, I encourage you to share your experience and your findings in appropriate ways with your colleagues. If some or all mainstream publications of the mental health profession may possibly eschew this subject or your findings, there are certainly viable alternatives.

This book represents one. Call, write or e-mail me.

Book Two awaits your involvement.

Bibliography and Suggested Reading:

To Hell & Back, Maurice Rawlings, M.D.; Thomas Nelson Publishers, Nashville

Reunions, Raymond Moody, M.D. with Paul Perry; Villard Books

Spirit Releasement Therapy: A Technique Manual, William J. Baldwin, Ph.D.; Headline Books, Inc.

UFOs in the New Age, William M. Alnor; Baker Book House

Beyond The Brain, Stanislav Grof; SUNY Press

The Alien Agenda, Dr. Clifford Wilson; Signet

Gods of Air and Darkness, Richard E. Mooney; Fawcett

The Complete Guide to Mysterious Beings, John Keel; Doubleday

Brother Termite, Patricia Anthony; Ace

Symbols, Signs & Signets, Ernst Lehner; Dover Books

Futureman, Robert C. Girard; Arcturus Books

The Gospel of Life (Evangelium Vitae), Pope John Paul II; Times Books

The Gospel According to Jesus, Stephen Mitchell; HarperCollins Publishers

The Believer's Guide to Spiritual Warfare, Thomas B. White; Servant Publications

Shouting At The Wolf, Anderson Reed; Citadel Press

The History of the Devil, Paul Carus; Open Court Publishing Co.

Unmasking the Enemy, Nelson S. Pacheco and Tommy Blann; Bendan Press

Grand Illusions, Dr. Gregory L. Little; White Buffalo Books

The Poltergeist Experience, D. Scott Rogo; Penguin Books

Possessed: The True Story of an Exorcism, Thomas B. Allen; Bantam Books

West Virginia UFOs: Close Encounters in the Mountain State, Bob Teets; Headline Books, Inc. (contains "Matrix of UFO Beliefs" by Dick Farley)

The Stalk, Janet and Chris Morris; ROC

Cosmic Patriot Files (Vol. 1 & 2); Abelard Productions, Inc.

The Mind of God, Paul Davies; Touchstone (Simon & Schuster)

Alien Identities, Richard L. Thompson; Govardhan Hill Publishing

The Unquiet Dead, Dr. Edith Fiore; Ballantine Books

Revelation, David Bischoff; Warner Books

The Way of the Shaman, Michael Harner; Harper SanFrancisco

Soul Retrieval, Sandra Ingerman; HarperSanFrancisco

The Origins of Satan, Elaine Pagels; Random House

Book (title unknown); T. L. Osborn

The Dilemma of Psychology, Lawrence LeShan, Ph.D.; Dutton

The Disuniting of America, Arthur M. Schlesinger, Jr.,

The Edge of Evil, Jerry Johnson; Word Publishing

all of Dr. Jacques Vallee's books...

The Bible

The Book of Enoch, the 19th Century translation by Lawrence

Aliens Discussions, Proceedings of the 1992 MIT Abduction Study Conference, Andrea & David Pritchard, John Mack, et al, eds. 1995, North

Cambridge Press.

Seth Speaks: The Eternal Validity of the Soul, Jane Roberts; Seth publishers

E.T. 101, Mission Control and JHO; Harper SanFrancisco

The Aquarian Conspiracy, Marilyn Ferguson, Jeremy P. Tarcher/Perigee Books, New York

Secret Life: First Hand Accounts of UFO Abductions, David M. Jacobs, Ph.D., Simon and Schuster, New York

Millennium Prophecies, Stephen Skinner, Longmeadow Press, Stamford, CT

The American Warrior, Chris Morris and Janet Morris, Longmeadow Press, Stamford, CT

A Dictionary of Angels, including the fallen angels, Gustav Davidson, The Free Press (div. of Macmillan, Inc.) New York

The Continuum Encyclopedia of Symbols, Udo Becker (ed.), Continuum Publishing Company, New York

Modern Hypnosis: Theory and Practice, Masud Ansari, Ph.D., Mas-Press, Washington, D.C.

Communion: A True Story, Whitley Strieber, Avon Books, New York

Ibn Taymeeyah's Essay on The Jinn (Demons), Abu Ameenah Bilal Philips (trans.), Tawheed Publications, Riyadh, Saudi Arabia

Intruders: The Incredible Visitations at Copley Woods, Budd Hopkins, Ballantine Books, New York

Unholy Alliance, Peter Levenda, Avon Books, New York

Journeys Out Of The Body, Robert A. Monroe, Doubleday & Company, New York

Star Born, Brad Steiger and Sherry Hansen Steiger, Berkley Books, New York

Remote Viewers: The Secret History of America's Psychic Spies, Jim Schnabel, Dell Publishing, New York

Man-Made UFOs 1944-1994: 50 Years of Suppression, Renato Vesco & David Hatcher Childress, Adventures Unlimited Press, Stelle, IL

Underground Bases and Tunnels: What is the government trying to hide?, Richard Sauder, Ph.D. Dracon Press, Abingdon, VA

Invisible Residents, Ivan T. Sanderson, Avon, NY

Starseed: The Third Millennium, Ken Carey, Harper, San Francisco

Aliens Among Us, Ruth Montgomery, Fawcett Crest, NY

Encounters, Edith Fiore, Ph.D., Ballantine Books, NY

Window of Opportunity, Newt Gingrich, Tom Doherty Associates, NY

Extra-Terrestrials Among Us, George C. Andrews, Llewellyn Publications, MN

Index

W

About The Author

Bob Teets won more than 30 state and national press awards as a West Virginia journalist in the 1980s, then founded Headline Books, Inc., a private book publishing firm, where he continues to serve as President and Managing Editor.

To date, Mr. Teets has personally interviewed more than 2,500 American UFO percipients. Highlights of these interviews and current UFO news is included in *The American UFO Newsletter*, a bi-monthly publication which Mr. Teets edits. He obtained a B.S. in journalism from West Virginia University, is a trained hypnotherapist (M.Ht.) and Spirit Releasement Therapy practitioner in private practice.

Earlier works by Mr. Teets include many regional titles in addition to the compilation newsbook, *Killing Waters*, declared a *USA Today* best-seller.

He resides with his wife and daughter in the Appalachian Mountains.